FROM NAPOLEON TO STALIN

FROM NAPOLEON
TO STALIN

COMMENTS ON EUROPEAN HISTORY

BY

A. J. P. TAYLOR

Fellow of Magdalen College, Oxford

HAMISH HAMILTON
LONDON

PRINTED IN GREAT BRITAIN BY
LOWE AND BRYDONE (PRINTERS) LIMITED, LONDON, N.W.10

TO
A. P. W.

CONTENTS

INTRODUCTION

THE pieces collected here span the century and a half
from the French Revolution to the present day. For the
most part I did not choose the subjects; they chose me.
What I offer are echoes from the past, called forth by a
centennial occasion or by the publication of some book of
memoirs. All the same there is an underlying theme. It is
the theme which has run through European history since
the French Revolution—the search for stability in an unstable
world. The great revolution destroyed tradition as the basis
for society; ever since men have been seeking for something
to take its place. Napoleon was an early attempt at a solution
—at once continuing the revolution and ending it, embodying
French Nationalism and yet attempting to set up a single
European State. Stalin, at the end of the period, shows the
same contrast—the revolutionary who has become the man
of authority or, in less personal terms, the revolution which
has itself become a tradition and a dogma. For Marxism has
carried to an extreme the rationalism of the French Revolution;
yet (as the personal experience of the final essay shows) will
no longer tolerate the free play of intellect.

The French Revolution challenged the established social
order; equally it upset the established order of states. Though
the traditional Balance of Power proved strong enough to
defeat Napoleon, it was itself sapped from within by the rise
of Nationalism, especially of German Nationalism. This is a
curious outcome. The defenders of the old order, such as
Gentz, supposed that their main concern would be "the
French problem." Instead we have had "the German problem"
on our hands for half a century and, but for Bismarck, would
have had it even earlier. France, originator of the upheaval,
has become the most defensive of the Great Powers, a development perhaps exaggerated here by the accidental concentration
on the period immediately before 1939. The age of German
power may now be over and the role of tyrant of Europe may

have passed from West to East, from Napoleon to Stalin. In that case, the spirit of national independence will have new tasks and new enemies; this is my excuse for ending, not irrelevantly, with the dispute between Marshal Tito and orthodox Communism.

This collection may give a misleading impression of my attitude to "the Russian problem." In 1945 and 1946 I discussed this question in various talks on current affairs which I gave for the British Broadcasting Corporation. These talks ended when they were described by Mr. Herbert Morrison in the House of Commons as "anti-British, anti-American, and not particularly competent."[1] I would have liked to give the reader a chance of confirming Mr. Morrison's judgment; but when I looked at these talks again they seemed too dated to stand reprinting. All the same I should not like it to be thought that I was ashamed of the opinions which I then expressed. I still think that the alienation of the Soviet Union after the second German war was in part the fault of the Western Powers. First we were sentimental in Russia's favour; then we were sentimental against her. I would have preferred hard, though fair, bargaining, a preference founded, I think, on past experience. At any rate I thought there was a use for a historian who would discuss Russian and Communist aims with the same detachment as he would discuss anything else. The B.B.C. thought otherwise; they wanted those who would expound "the British way of life." I hope never to be numbered in this band of secular missionaries.

I have to express my thanks to the editors, publishers and proprietors of the *Manchester Guardian*, the *New Statesman and Nation*, *The Times Literary Supplement* and *Critique*, for permission to reprint material which first appeared in the pages of these periodicals. *1848: Opening of an Era* was written as introduction to the volume of the same name, published by Allan Wingate. *Trieste* was written in 1945 at the request of the Yugoslav Government.

A. J. P. T.

[1] *Hansard*, 431. H.C. Deb. 1285.

PART ONE

HISTORICAL

I

NAPOLEON

(1) *On Himself*

A LIFE of Napoleon written by himself! The appeal seems
irresistible. Mr. de Chair, the editor,[1] describes it as
"the voice of the giant himself." The conversation of giants,
then, must be very dull. The proclamations and bulletins of
Napoleon show him to have been a propagandist of genius;
so, too, was Goebbels. Yet the Memoirs of the one are as
dreary as the Diaries of the other. In fact, the Memoirs of
Napoleon—undoubtedly a genuine product of his mind—
convinced me that the Goebbels' diaries were genuine; if
Napoleon could write as boringly as this, Goebbels could
also. Both works are, of course, full of lies; that was to be
expected. It is the drabness, the fatuity, the commonplaceness
of mind, that are surprising. What, for instance, could be
more idiotic than Napoleon's explanation of polygamy in his
chapter on Egypt? It occurs, he says, in countries inhabited
by men of several colours and "is the only means of preventing
them persecuting each other," since every man can have a
black wife, a white one, a copper-coloured one "and one of
some other colour." He proceeds to recommend it in the
French colonies as the solution of the colour question, so that
every man can have "one white, one black, and one Mulatto
wife, at the same time."

Napoleon knew well that he was not a brilliant author;
and he protected himself by speaking contemptuously of
writers, as he did of his other enemies. Just as he described
the English as "men who were continually at table, almost
always intoxicated, and of uncommunicative disposition," so
he dismissed writers as men of no practical sense.

He was not concerned to compete with those detestable

---

[1] *Napoleon's Memoirs.* Edited by Somerset de Chair.

13

ideologues; he had no interest at all in creating a work of art—his life in action had been creation enough. His reminiscences were written, or rather dictated, for effect. They were to launch a legend, the legend of Divine Caesar. Cold and aloof like a marble statue in classical robes, they are without personality; and it was a great error of judgment by Mr. de Chair to substitute the first person singular for "Napoleon," "the Emperor," "the general" of the original text. For Napoleon's statue is not vocal even after the fashion of the statue in *Don Giovanni*; and the essential purpose of these writings is in their remoteness from life. Napoleon the man was finished; Napoleon the institution had to be perpetuated.

It is not surprising therefore that the only section of Memoirs which Napoleon completed and finally polished is the part dealing with the campaign of Waterloo. A defeat of such finality needs a good deal of explaining away. Napoleon had an excuse in Grouchy's failure to come up with Blücher on June 18; and he repeats this excuse again and again. But he is pulled up by an uneasy sense that the real failure lay in the faulty orders which Grouchy received from his Supreme Commander; and Napoleon swings off on the other tack that Waterloo was an indecisive battle, the effect of which could have been undone by a further campaign. This line, too, has its dangers; for the failure to continue the war could be explained only by the war-weariness of the French. This was not an argument with which to appeal to posterity. The only way out is to assert that his strategy was throughout correct and that Wellington and Blücher committed "every conceivable mistake." Thus Napoleon persuaded himself that he had in fact won the battle of Waterloo and his Memoirs end with an expression of sympathy for the people of London "when they learnt of the catastrophe which had befallen their army."

The main section of the record, which runs from the siege of Toulon to the battle of Marengo, lacks the finish of the Waterloo narrative. Napoleon dictated these chapters haphazard to two amanuenses; and the two rivals kept their work separate when they published it after Napoleon's death. Mr. de Chair has sorted out the two sources and pruned away the asides with which Napoleon relieved the tedium. In this story of his early success Napoleon had less to explain away; all the same he never missed a chance to heighten the emphasis on the unique character and achievement of "the Emperor." Thus Paoli, the Corsican patriot, "used frequently to say of the young artillery officer [myself], 'He is a man for a Plutarch's biography.'" With this unlikely anecdote Napoleon blots out the story of his equivocal behaviour in Corsican affairs. Entertaining, too, in their way are the passages on naval warfare, in which Napoleon proves that it is much easier to win battles at sea than on land; Trafalgar is successfully rubbed out of existence. But for the most part the principles of Plutarch are observed all too seriously. There are accounts of Italy and Egypt which could have been taken from any gazeteer; even the military narrative lacks spirit. This served Napoleon's purpose. "The general" remained without a rival figure; and Napoleon could conclude with an account of Marengo, which conceals that he had lost the battle and slides, almost without mention, over Desaix who had come to Bonaparte's rescue. It is a fitting end to a narrative which is unreliable from beginning to end.

Can Napoleon have supposed that this dull and lying record would really secure his fame? This puzzle is the only point of interest raised by this book. Some part of the explanation may be found in the decline of his faculties. The only exciting passages are the quotations from the proclamations which Bonaparte wrote as the young general of the Army of Italy; these still ring with life, and their author could not have written dully however hard he tried. Success corrupts; and Napoleon had achieved success without parallel in modern history. The spare, beautiful artillery officer had become fat and coarse; and his mind became coarse at the same time. Besides, Napoleon had expected everyone to sacrifice himself for the Empire; and the first sacrifice had been his own personality. The young Bonaparte had been vital, though no doubt unattractive; Napoleon had squeezed the life out of him. Flashes of personality persisted, even at St. Helena. These make Napoleon interesting to history; they did not interest Napoleon himself. He was concerned only with his public performance. Stendhal found the key to Napoleon, when he described Julien Sorel, after his first night with Mme. de Rênal, asking himself: "*Ai-je bien joué mon rôle?*" Sorel, like Napoleon, was dominated by ambition; he lacked inner life and so fails to hold the reader's sympathy or even attention. Napoleon's was a more complicated case. He had begun as a romantic figure in the spirit of Rousseau; he ended as an abstraction from Plutarch. To use the clumsy contemporary phrase, this destruction of Napoleon by himself was the last triumph of the Classical over the Romantic. The essence of the Romantic movement was the elevation of individual sentiment and of individual character; yet Napoleon, with a more remarkable character than any, was ashamed of possessing it and returned to a Classical worship of the external world.

The explanation of this outmoded artificiality is simple; and Napoleon himself hints at it in the early pages of his Memoirs. He could have been genuine—"romantic"—only as a Corsican patriot; once he deserted his natural cause, he could only play parts and to do this he had to crush out his individuality. Sometimes, as when he played at being a French patriot or even a French Emperor, the part came off; at others, as when he played at being a Moslem in Egypt or wished to play at being the liberator-general after Waterloo, the pretence was too blatant. But, for a man who claimed to possess a sense of reality, Napoleon's judgment was strangely unreliable from start to finish. The eighteenth of Brumaire was as wild an adventure as the Hundred Days; in neither case did Napoleon have any clear idea what he was doing—he was simply "playing his role." For that matter Marengo was as much a gamble as Waterloo. It implanted in Napoleon the belief that he had truly mastered the external world; this gave him the necessary self-confidence for his career, though it ultimately brought him to disaster. Traditional ideas and traditional institutions had lost their force. Losing faith in God, men sought a human saviour. The first of these human gods was Napoleon; and the condition of his fame was the confident readiness to attempt the impossible. Napoleon believed in himself; he continued to believe even when reality had shattered the basis of this belief, and he supposed that others would believe too. Hence he even believed that readers could be found for his Memoirs.

All the same, despite Napoleon, a human being is buried in these writings. Napoleon no doubt thought that he was building a monument to his future fame. Most of the time, in reality, he was fighting his battles over again simply for the pleasure of it; and this time without risk of failure. No reader can be persuaded that the catalogue of divisions and the description of obscure skirmishes serve any literary purpose. Napoleon had ceased to think of the reader. He had escaped from the unpleasant reality of St. Helena and was manœuvring imaginary armies. There once more he could exercise the devotion to detail and the implacable demands for speed that had been the secret of his success (though also of his failure). Bending over the map of Lombardy, he could once more forget that Josephine had been unfaithful to him immediately after marriage (and he expected the reader to forget it too). In fact, if only he exerted his will strongly enough, he might again master the external world: St. Helena would disappear and Lombardy, or Paris under the Consulate, become once more reality. It was this belief in the human will, at any rate his own, that made Napoleon the representative and culmination of the French Revolution.

The essence of the Revolution was belief in man. Once you believe that man is naturally good, you must believe, too, that he can do anything. Napoleon certainly held this belief about himself. And no doubt man can do anything, if he goes the right way about it. The right way, as the events of the last century and a half have shown, is the way of science: the improvement of technique. The men of the French Revolution, and Napoleon with them, supposed that they could master the world by will alone. Hence the Napoleonic armies, for example, marched faster than other armies simply by the compelling force of Napoleon's command; modern armies move faster by train or aeroplane. Napoleon killed his secretaries by over-work; with the dictaphone and the type-writer they would have survived quite easily. Napoleon was following the wrong course; the further his will carried him, the greater was bound to be his final catastrophe. He supposed that events could be made; in the end events took their revenge on him. There was no essential difference between Napoleon in victory and in defeat (hence his own bewilderment at Waterloo): he always asked the impossible, and sometimes it was granted him. This is the real basis of the Napoleonic legend (as it will be for the legend of Hitler). Napoleon is the hero of all those who resent reality, of all those who will not trouble to master "the art of the possible." Napoleon is the supreme example of the human being who became more than life-size; and those who admire Napoleon are really flattering the human being in themselves. Yet what did this wonderful human being end in? A querulous sick man on a sub-tropical island dictating a drab and meaningless record to wile away the time. The Memoirs of Napoleon suggest that there is something to be said for not thinking that you are God.

(2) The Verdict of History

Events are well enough in their way; what historians write about them is much better. Who really cares about the later Roman Emperors, about Dutch William, or even about Pericles? These survive by grace of Gibbon, Macaulay and Thucydides. The greatest figure of modern times made himself such by providing a myth which would provide endless fascination for historians. Napoleon knew the secret of survival: *quel roman que ma vie!* His own literary gifts were those of an amateur—characteristic of one who carried that second-rate tear-jerker, *The Sorrows of Werther*, in his hip-pocket; the Napoleonic legend would never have taken hold had it depended on Napoleon's own writings. Napoleon's great stroke was to provide raw material for works of genius, so that French historians wrote about Napoleon inevitably, as every Greek playwright interpreted the story of the Trojan wars. Of course there is always a certain amount to be discovered about Napoleon, as no doubt matter of archæological interest can be found by grubbing in the ruins of Troy. But the profundities of the human spirit are to be found in what men have made of the legend, not in the archives and the rubble. The career of Napoleon is the greatest of modern legends.

This fact, once noticed, seems obvious and inescapable; and it is surprising that no one has had the idea long ago of discussing what French writers have made of Napoleon. To discover the obvious which no one else has thought of is the speciality of Professor Geyl,[1] one of the great historical minds of our time. It would be unfair to say that he demolishes the reputations of the great French historians; though he exposes their flaws, there remains, in his words "what life and energy, what creative power, what ingenuity, imagination and daring!" These words are a reminder of peculiar value for the English reader. Every continental student of history, even if he be a German, knows that the French are the greatest practitioners of the art. English historians have never recovered from the fraud put over on us by Acton (or perhaps Carlyle) and still suppose that serious history—scientific history as it is called —was perfected in Germany. But what tawdry stuff the German historians are compared to the stars of Professor Geyl's book—and how long-winded!

Professor Geyl gives a plain analysis of what French historians from the Restoration to the present day have written about Napoleon. He starts with Chateaubriand and ends with Georges Lefebvre. Each writer is summarized with the painstaking detachment with which a newspaper correspondent gives a summary of the foreign press. There are no graces of style, no novelty in the point of view; the general effect is humdrum, almost dull. It is like listening to a conversation where tones are never raised, where there is never a flicker of emphasis nor even, one supposes, of interest. As the conversation proceeds, it gradually becomes clear that Professor Geyl, far from being the club bore, declines to raise his voice simply because he is discussing the most profound topics of human experience. It is rare enough to find a work of history which is interesting, let alone exciting. This book is vastly more, an infinite consolation to the professional historian: it shows that history is a subject which can provoke thought. For my part,

[1] *Napoleon: For and Against.* By Pieter Geyl.

I would rather have written Professor Geyl's book than invented Existentialism or the new fashion in academic philosophy—what is it called? The subject, at any rate, which now spends its time debating whether it was once correct to describe itself as logical positivism. Professor Geyl's book enables the historian to look the philosopher in the face without cringing for quite a week.

His book teaches one, in the first place, a great deal about Napoleon. French historians have found in Napoleon infinite variety; and all of it was there. It is impossible to read this catalogue of their judgments without realizing that Napoleon really was a most extraordinary man, probably the most extraordinary figure that has ever appeared in the world of politics. Sorel saw him as the man who devoted his life to the defence of the natural frontiers; Bourgeois as the man who lived only for the creation of a great Empire of the Middle East; Driault as the restorer of the Roman Empire in Europe, the greatest of the Caesars; Vandal even discovered in him the pacifier of the world—no wonder he spoke of "the ultimate justice and grandeur of his aim." The same variety and the same vastness are revealed in the descriptions of Napoleon's work as a civilian ruler—the heir of the Revolution, the restorer of order, the architect of the Code Napoleon, the founder of the French Empire, the protector of the Catholic Church. All these things happened in Napoleon's time; yet the cumulative effect of them is not to increase admiration for Napoleon, rather to rouse doubts.

Here Professor Geyl, as it were, turns the tables on Napoleon: for his book, despite its cool tone and its scholarship, is an anti-Napoleonic tract, the most formidable ever composed. He has given the legend a good showing in order to show that it is a legend, that it over-reaches itself by its very absurdity. He quotes the rhetoric of Thiers, the brilliance of Vandal, the sophistication of Sorel; then brings them to earth with a gentle query—the murder of the Duke of Enghien? the breach of the Treaty of Amiens? the oppression and exploitation of Europe? the stifling of French Liberalism? Above all, the lies, the intrigues, the dishonesty? Professor Geyl has no doubt of his own verdict:

He was a conqueror with whom it was impossible to live; who could not help turning an ally into a vassal or at least interpreting the relationship to his own exclusive advantage; who decorated his lust of conquest with the fine-sounding phrases of progress and civilization; and who at last, in the name of the whole of Europe, which was to look to him for order and peace presumed to brand England as the universal disturber and enemy.

This is not, however, only the verdict of a dispassionate Dutch observer. The historians of the legend do not exhaust French writings on Napoleon. Indeed, all Professor Geyl's criticism of the admirers of Napoleon is based on the work of French scholars; and his analysis of the two attitudes, *for* and *against*, is a splendid contribution to the study of French ideas. The cleavage is, in the first place, political. In England admiration for Napoleon has often (perhaps usually) been found on the "left"—a line running from Lady Holland to Hilaire Belloc and (dare I say it?) Bernard Shaw. What English admirers of Napoleon have in common is simple: they are all "agin the government" and, since Napoleon was also against the British Government, they suppose that he was on their side. In France, however, the "establishment" has been on the left, especially in the time of the Third Republic; and Napoleon has been the hero of the Conservatives. They did not need to pretend that Napoleon cared for liberty: they were delighted that he had destroyed it and wished to follow his example. They echoed the phrase of Barrès: "Napoleon, Teacher of Energy," and praised, perhaps exaggerated, those qualities which made Napoleon the precursor of Fascism. Moreover, unlike English writers, they did not conceal that Napoleon was the enemy of England, not merely of the British Government; for, since England represented the principles of liberty, of constitutional government, and of agreement between the nations, she was their enemy also. This tradition, though strong, was the school of a minority in France. French writers who cared for liberty, who opposed militarism, had no illusions about Napoleon and exposed the errors of those who had. French Liberals in the nineteenth century, and Socialists in the twentieth, stood unanimously for "the other France" which repudiated Napoleon with his gospel of energy and violence.

The cleavage *for* and *against*, as well as being political, is

also professional; this is a point of peculiar interest fully
worked out by Professor Geyl. The men of letters, with the
exception of Taine, have been for Napoleon, and Taine was
only against Napoleon because he recognized in Napoleon
himself; the men of learning have been against him. The
men of letters have often been distinguished scholars, as
Vandal and Sorel were; but, in the last resort, they were
concerned to produce an effect, to write a work of literary
genius. It is a very different Napoleon who appears in the
school text-books. Indeed one is almost driven to postulate
the general rule: the better written a book, the more unreliable
as history. But there is more in it than that. Tocqueville said
of Napoleon: "He was as great as a man can be without
morality"; and the truth is that all men of letters, that is all
who care for good writing, are, in this sense, immoral. They
will always subordinate reality to effect and facts to phrases.
Paine's judgment on Burke will serve for every French writer
on Napoleon whose works one reads for pleasure: "He pities
the plumage but forgets the dying bird." Nothing is stranger
than the delusion of our time that men of letters are, by nature,
champions of political, or even of intellectual liberty. If
Professor Geyl's book is not evidence enough to the contrary,
consider the famous writers who made the pilgrimage to
Mussolini. Of course, scientists are even worse—but then
one hardly expects political sense from them. It was only
when reading Professor Geyl's book that I realized that
professors of history, at any rate in France, are so much better.
Their record of integrity has been almost unbroken. Even in
the Second Empire the committee of scholars, employed to
publish the correspondence of Napoleon I, was too resolutely
honest to please Napoleon III; it had to be replaced in 1864
by a committee of literary men (including Sainte-Beuve)
which set out to publish only what Napoleon "would have
made available to the public if he had wished to display
himself and his system to posterity." Still, the achievement of
the French professional historians cannot necessarily be
counted to the general credit of the trade. What German
historian stood out against the cult of Bismarck, at any rate
until Bismarck had failed? And what chance is there that any

German historian will stand out against the coming cult of
Hitler? As for English historians, they have hardly escaped
from the Anglican sycophancy which marked the universities
until the beginning of this century. Chaplains of the pirate
ship, they have extolled the British Empire as persistently as
the French men of letters extolled the Empire of Napoleon.
The French professors represented a general "university"
culture which hardly exists outside France. As Professor
Geyl says: "The scholarliness of their method . . . disciplines
their mental attitude. But it would be foolish to overlook the
fact that these authors came to Napoleon with their own, with
different, *a priori* ideas, that they measure him against standards
of spiritual freedom, of culture, of humanity, of social progress,
that politically they are as a rule of the left. With some of them
anti-clericalism is predominant, with others liberalism, or
socialism." What a wonderful country of which these things
can be said of university professors!

The last quotation is a reminder that Geyl's book, as well
as being a book about Napoleon and about French historians,
is about clerical values (using the word in Benda's sense).
Geyl concludes his praise of the professional historian, Georges
Lefebvre, in whom he finds the most convincing version of
Napoleon, with criticism: "I should like to see the eternal
postulates of respect for the human personality, of the feeling
for spiritual freedom, of lofty idealism, of truthfulness, taken
into account when the final reckoning is made." This is a
startling evocation of the shade of Acton; and it leaves me
wondering whether the virtues of a historian and those of a
"clerk" are the same after all.

II

NAPOLEON AND GENTZ

How has the continent of Europe escaped political unification? Everything in Europe seems to call for it; everything, that is, except the temperament and traditions of its peoples. More uniform in climate than China, less diverse in religion than India, less diverse in race than the United States of America, Europe has had for centuries a single culture and a common social structure. Landowner and peasant, merchant and banker, factory owner and factory worker, artist and scholar, would nowhere find themselves in an alien world in moving from one part of the Continent to another. There is a European way of thinking and of living; even a uniform pattern of meals—England and Russia, both outside the Continent, are both marked off from it by their times for eating. For a thousand years men have dreamed of European union; yet for a thousand years this most uniform of continents has defied political unification. The most recent attempt at it we have just lived through and successfully opposed; and it is too soon, perhaps, to estimate the historical place of Hitler's New Order. Yet as it slips into history we can already begin to see how little of it was original, how much of it (like most German political activity) a perverse aping of an earlier French achievement. Hitler was Napoleon's Caliban. The French came as liberators and offered to Europe far more than did their German imitators; yet in the Napoleonic Empire, too, appear the defects—one is tempted to say the inevitable defects—of attempting to force Europe into a single political mould.

"L'Empire de Napoléon,"[1] of which M. Madelin writes, is the Empire of 1811, the year of calm and grandeur before the great storm which was to blow the Empire out of exist-

---

[1] *Histoire du Consulat et de l'Empire.* X. L'Empire de Napoléon. By Louis Madelin.

ence, the year when the Empire extended from the Baltic
to the confines of Greece. It was, above all, the year of the
dynasty. The Austrian marriage had already announced
Napoleon's changed role from that of the continuator of the
revolution to that of the champion of monarchical order
against "the disorderly spirit" of the *canaille*; with the birth
of a son he became the originator of the Holy Alliance.
Previously Napoleon's sentiment had been for his brothers
and sisters—the family sentiment of a Corsican. Now the
thrones of the Bonapartes were endangered—Louis dismissed
from Holland, even Joseph given only a breathing-space in
Spain. Napoleon imagined that he had founded a dynasty
and had become indeed the successor of Louis XIV. Yet,
with the strange realism which redeemed the vulgarity of his
character, he saw through his own pretences. He said to
Molé: "We are the monarchy of a week"; and, again: "All
this will last as long as I do, but, after me, my son will perhaps
think himself fortunate if he has 40,000 livres in the funds."
Sometimes he consoled himself with the thought that his son,
"probably an ordinary man, of moderate gifts," would be
"the constitutional King *tout trouvé*"; for Napoleon knew
that "in the long run, the sword is always vanquished by the
spirit"; that he himself had had neither time nor patience to
build up a new system of institutions.

But Napoleon refused to be shaken by his own scepticism.
He accepted his destiny. The revolution had repudiated the
legacy of history and had made the gigantic attempt to build
a system of social life on the basis of abstract principles.
Napoleon, profoundly sceptical and deeply experienced in
practical affairs, knew well that society could not be based
on reason alone; the only alternative he could hit upon was
trickery. He invented institutions in which he did not believe,
but which he was naïve enough to suppose would deceive
others. His own imperial title, the new nobility, the weari-
some court ceremonial (imitated from the German courts,
not from Versailles)—even these tawdry pretences were given
a false animation by the energy with which Napoleon threw
himself into the masquerade. Lacking belief and lacking
purpose, Napoleon tried to solve all his problems by the same

means: ever more activity. As long as he kept driving forward and driving others forward, he could hope to escape the failure which his own mind told him to be inevitable. Hence the pell-mell of ideas, which made Narbonne exclaim: "What a man! What great ideas! What dreams! Where is the keeper of this genius? The whole thing is scarcely credible. We are between Bedlam and the Panthéon." Hence, too, by 1811 the weariness which overcame Napoleon, even occasionally the longing for an obscure family life which made him so much exaggerate the virtues of the dumpy Marie Louise.

Napoleon's latest invention was the Empire of the West, with its second capital at Rome. But this led him inevitably into conflict with the Papacy and so to the destruction of his most genuinely conservative work, the Concordat. Napoleon believed the Catholic religion to be useful for his Empire; he was *plus catholique encore que chrétien*. The French hierarchy owed their security and greatness to Napoleon; good Bona-partists, the last thing they wanted was to quarrel with the Emperor. Yet they, too, had to follow the logic of their position. At the Council of Imperial Bishops Napoleon's own creations, even his uncle the Cardinal Fesch, were driven reluctantly and feebly, but inescapably, to adopt the attitude of martyrs. The quarrel with the Church was the final proof that a con-servative system could not be built on reason and human energy. The Empire, at its height, had no convinced supporters —not even Napoleon. The régime was composed of all those who had profited from the Empire; but they supported it only so long as they could enjoy their profits, and would turn against it the moment that it demanded sacrifices from them. Napoleon had tried to make a collective system out of individual interests; he could not blame the deserters of 1814. Not that there was opposition in 1811. Talleyrand, the wisest man in France, and perhaps Fouché, waited for the blunder which they knew that even Napoleon would make; but for the most part men dared not look into the future.

The most fortunate were the younger men who had not yet made their fortunes and to whom had fallen the administra-tion of the Empire outside France. Here ceaseless activity, ceaseless levelling, still seemed a substitute for genuine creation. Since there could be only one form of rational government and since that government had been achieved in France, all Europe was to be remade on the French pattern. Napoleon himself defined the aim of Imperial policy: "I must have a European code, a European Court of Cassation, a common coinage, common weights and measures, and common laws; I have to make of all the peoples of Europe one single people, and of Paris the capital of the world." Fontanes, the head of the University, put it more dramatically: "We must be able to say: 'At this very moment all the students of the Empire are at work on the same Latin passage.'" The first stage of French government was liberation—the destruction of privileges, of abuses, of traditional inefficiency. It was welcomed with gratitude by the people and with enthusiasm by the local philosophers. Hegel, ever an admirer of successful power, wrote of Imperial rule: "It is enough that it be the will of Heaven, that is, of the French Emperor." By 1811 this first stage was past. The peoples, liberated from the old, were being driven into the new; and they were stiffening their backs. All over Europe the Imperial system was sticking in the mud of human reluctance to be turned into perfect beings; and, from Napoleon downwards, human energy flagged and faltered.

M. Madelin is puzzled by the failure of the French system to take roots. For the failure of a rational system he seeks a rational cause. Conscription and the continental system, he concludes, were the two disadvantages which outweighed the benefits. Yet these seem to him rather forced on Napoleon by the wilful opposition of England and Russia than springing inevitably from the Napoleonic system. It shocks him that Napoleon should have declared his principle to be *La France avant tout*; but it shocks him even more that the peoples of Europe should have been reluctant to have their lives run for them by the French. M. Madelin concludes that they would have got used to Napoleon with time: "It was only time that he lacked." But time was lacking for what? Only to organize an even greater catastrophe. Tocqueville was wiser. He said of Napoleon: "He was as great as a man can be without morality." What Napoleon and his Empire lacked was not

time, still less energy, but belief. Frenchmen can rule with
grace and France had a real civilization to offer; therefore
Napoleon's rule was more tolerable than Hitler's. But,
ultimately, it broke against the same obstacle: the unwillingness of European peoples to be fitted into a uniform system.

The Imperial cause did not even inspire the French.
The reality in the Napoleonic Empire was French national
consciousness; and Napoleon, thinking to found the United
States of Europe, became in fact the greatest of French
national heroes. The national pride of France pointed the
way which the rest of Europe would follow. The great revolution of 1789, with its rationalistic philosophy, did not transform
the French into Europeans but made them more assertively
French. Throughout Europe the French were successful in
destroying the traditional order; and even where they did not
conquer, that order destroyed itself by its rigidity and decay.
The outcome was the rise of nationalism in Europe, the only
way, once historical differences were lost, by which men could
be different. The rejection of uniformity was the one thing
uniform to the inhabitants of Europe. This conclusion,
implicit in the fall of the Napoleonic Empire, has been
emphasized again after Hitler's New Order. Unexampled
destruction has been followed by unexampled nationalism.
And by a simple process: when men lose everything, the
nation remains their sole possession.

Europe could not be brought together by destruction and
by the rule of a single people, either in Napoleon's time or in
Hitler's. But could there not be another way—the way of
preserving something of the historic forms and bringing men
together in voluntary co-operation? This great question is
asked now, as it was asked in the age preceding and following
the fall of Napoleon. This question dominated the mind of
Metternich and led him to devise the "system Metternich."
It dominated, too, the mind of the man from whom Metternich
learned his system, Friedrich von Gentz[1] (the noble title was a
gift from the legitimist King of Sweden), a man who with

---

[1] *Secretary of Europe.* The Life of Friedrich Gentz, Enemy of Napoleon. By
Golo Mann. Translated by William H. Woglom. *Friedrich von Gentz.* Defender
of the Old Order. By Paul R. Sweet.

many human faults had probably the most interesting mind of his day. Vain, snobbish, a cadger and a spendthrift, Gentz was the first great commentator on current affairs; and the heart of anyone who has ever attempted that speculative role must warm to him in success and still more in failure. His two biographers sort out the facts of his life; both fail to straighten out his ideas. And this is not surprising: Gentz would have been hard put to it to straighten them out himself. In 1814, when arguing against the deposition of Napoleon, he answered his own pamphlet against recognizing Napoleon, which he had written in 1804. What was more damaging, in 1820, when Gentz was advocating the censorship of the German Press, some German liberals reprinted the pamphlet against Press censorship which he had written in 1797. These inconsistencies are to Gentz's credit rather than the reverse. The enemy of perfectionist ideas, he sought the practical and the moderate: something that would not ask too much of human beings. Like Burke, though in even stormier times, he set habit against reason; or rather, tried to make a compromise between the two.

It is easiest to understand his opposition to Napoleon, though it made him for many years a solitary figure. Hegel, Goethe, all the great German figures of the day, expected Napoleon to make a new world for them. Only Gentz held from the start that nothing lasting could come from conquest and arbitrary rule. Napoleon was condemned to pursue ever greater success until it turned to failure; that was obvious afterwards, not so easy to predict in 1804 or even in 1807. But what cause should be set against the cause of the dictator? This was the search to which Gentz devoted his journalistic life, the question to which he never found a satisfactory answer. Certainly not the cause of German nationalism. This cause he dreaded even more than the cause of Napoleon. France, he believed, would, after defeat, come to accept an equal place among the Great Powers of Europe; in this belief he successfully advocated a peaceful policy towards Louis Philippe in 1830. But national Germany would be content with no place but the first: it would drive towards an even more perilous ascendancy than that of Napoleon and destroy

what remained of the European order. Gentz cared for historic
Germany and abandoned Prussia, the state of his birth, for
the more traditional Austria; he failed to see that this historic
Germany had been destroyed almost as much by the Habsburgs
as by Napoleon himself. War accelerates political developments; it does not cause them. In our own time the two
German wars have obscured the economic crisis which springs
everywhere from the rejection in men's minds of economic
individualism. So the Napoleonic wars obscured the political
crisis which sprang from the decay of traditional political
obligations. The restorations of 1815 were not real but sham-
Gothic.

Gentz at the end of his life confessed this. He said in
1830: "Were I to write the history of the last fifteen years, it
would be a continuous accusation of Metternich"; and he
condemned most strongly the steps which Metternich had
taken on his advice. The emptiness of the "system Metternich"
was made clear to Gentz by the Austrian restoration of absolutism in Naples after the revolution of 1821. The King of
the Two Sicilies was a *reductio ad absurdum* of legitimist
policy, just as the King of Greece is a *reductio ad absurdum* of
democratic policy a century or so later. Words and reality
were not in tune; and Gentz at least had the honesty to admit
it. After all, what could be more absurd than to preserve
irrational abuses on rational grounds? Once the political
institutions have become subject for argument, the traditional
must give way to the rational. Gentz came to admit this; he
only asked that the giving way should not be too rapid. Hence
he believed that both he, as a Conservative, and the Liberals
were doing a useful work; they demanded reforms—he slowed
them down. Like Canning opposing Parliamentary reform,
he thought that someone should defend the old order, even
when its destruction was certain.

In international affairs, too, Gentz came to admit that he
had defended "a lost cause." This lost cause was the Habsburg
monarchy; more deeply the cause of the historic European
States (including the Ottoman Empire); and most deeply of
all the cause of European union. During Gentz's lifetime
Europe had been offered the chance of union either under

Napoleon or against him. It took neither: Europe would not accept Napoleon's Empire, but failed to overthrow it. The liberation of Europe came from without, from England and Russia: Europe had been unable to solve its own problems or to determine its own destinies. European union demanded, and demands, co-operation between France and the principal Germanic Power, whatever name that may bear. But legitimist Austria would not accept the supremacy of Napoleon; liberal France would not work in partnership with Metternich's Austria; Stresemann's Germany would not take an equal place in the French order devised by Briand; and, least of all, will the France of the Fourth Republic become the junior partner of a revived Germany. The "good Europeans" who began with Gentz, Metternich and Talleyrand ended with Laval. Gentz saw the alternative; he regretted it, but believed that, like the victory of liberalism, it was inevitable. Europe failed to achieve her own union or freedom; therefore not union, but peace and a stable order of States had to be imposed from without. At the Congress of Westphalia all the Powers were European; at the Congress of Vienna the European Powers were three against two; now Europe has dwindled to a doubtful one among five.

Europe could not be united on a revolutionary programme; that was the lesson of the failure of Napoleon. Europe could not be united on a conservative programme; that was the lesson of the failure of Metternich and Gentz. Europe prized diversity; this had to be paid for by others. When Napoleon failed to cross the Channel, still more when the Grand Army perished in the snows of Russia, the fate of Europe passed from European hands: England and Russia became the trustees of European independence. In the nineteenth century the two trustees quarrelled over their private concerns; but, as 1914 and 1941 showed, they could not escape their trust. Now, as at all times since the Congress of Vienna, the security of Europe depends not on an impossible reconciliation between France and Germany, but on a lasting co-operation between England and Russia. The Congress system of Gentz's day was destroyed by Anglo-Russian disputes over Constantinople; the system of the United Nations would not

survive a second Crimean war. To reconcile British and
Russian interests in the Near East—this (as Metternich
realized after Gentz's death) was the essential condition for
European security. The passage of a century has only
reinforced the need.

III

1848

(1) *Year of Revolution*

"WE are making together the sublimest of poems."
Lamartine embodied the revolutions of 1848 in
speech and in deed; and his grandiose phrase was echoed
by every Radical in the revolutionary year. Heaven on earth
seemed nearer in 1848 than at any other moment in modern
history. Eighteen forty-eight was the link between the
centuries: it carried to the highest point the eighteenth-
century belief in the perfectibility of man, yet, all unexpectedly,
launched the social and national conflicts which ravage
Europe a century later. Socialism and Nationalism, as mass
forces, were both the product of 1848. The revolutions
determined the character of every country in Europe (except
Belgium) from the Pyrenees to the frontiers of the Russian
and Turkish empires; and these countries have since shown
common characteristics not shared by England, Russia, the
Balkans, or Scandinavia. Politically speaking, a "European"
is an heir of 1848.

The moment of the revolution was determined by the
financial crisis of 1846 and by bad harvests in 1846 and
1847. These caused food riots in the towns and sharpened
the long-standing grievances of the peasants in Eastern
Germany and in the Austrian Empire. Economic discontent
gave force to revolts; only the moral upheaval turned these
into a revolution. Eighteen forty-eight was the victory of
the "ideologues," as Napoleon had contemptuously named
them. Respect for traditional beliefs and forms of government
had broken down; as a German poet wrote, "Monarchy is
dead, though monarchs still live." Even the rulers had lost
faith in themselves. The King of Prussia received the revolutionary poet Herwegh in order to bow "before a worthy

C

opponent," and Metternich denounced "the rotten edifice" which it was his duty to uphold.

The revolutions repudiated "throne and altar"; equally they repudiated existing State frontiers and the treaty settlement of the Congress of Vienna. After forty years of peace and stability men were bored: they wished to translate into real life the poetry of Victor Hugo and the music of Berlioz. Most of the radical leaders were between thirty-five and forty years of age; they represented the generation which had caught only the echoes of the Napoleonic Empire and which wished to hear again through Europe the thunder of the guns —though this time on the barricades. The barricades, built in every city in Europe and often erected even when there was no fighting, were the symbol of 1848. The ideologues had evoked the masses for sixty years; in 1848 the masses at last took their call.

The ideas of 1848 were the ideas of the French Revolution, applied now without doubt or reserve. The men of 1789 had been concerned with freedom from arbitrary government and equality before the law; though they used democratic phrases they restricted "the people" to the property-owning middle class—even Robespierre only brought in the skilled artisan and petty shopkeeper. The men of 1848 had infinite faith in "the people," whom they identified with themselves; and every little radical club spoke for "the nation," as, say, the British Communist party speaks for the British "working class." The liberals, prizing the rights of 1789, saw these endangered by the intrusion of the masses and were thus driven on to the side of the counter-revolution; indeed, in most of Europe, the defeat of the revolution was achieved by liberals, to their own subsequent ruin. In the enmity between liberal and radical, too, 1848 created a political pattern peculiar to the continent of Europe.

Though the masses certainly broke on to the political stage, they did not fill the humble parts which had been allotted to them by the ideologues. The urban movements were revolts against hard conditions of life and work; caused not by the Industrial Revolution but by its absence. They were "Luddite" in character, seeking to destroy the new machines (especially seeking to destroy the railways which were being built by British capital and labour in western Europe). With the general increase of population, towns were growing; these, as yet, lacked the cheap goods of mass production which make urban life tolerable. The less industry, the more revolution. Belgium, the only industrialized country in Europe, escaped revolution; Italy, with no modern industry, had seven.

Marx, prophesying revolution for the rest of his life, was in fact foretelling the revolution of 1848 which he had experienced as a young man (prophets always foretell what has already happened); but he drew the wrong conclusion. Far from industrial development producing revolution, it was a protection against it; a century later the most advanced industrial countries are the least in danger from Communism. The urban masses of 1848 had no Socialist programme; they demanded "the right to work," the programme of Napoleon III and, subsequently, of Hitler. Their "social republic" was not Social Democracy; it was a longing for the days of mercantilism. Still, "the right to work" challenged "the rights of property," which had been the essential revolutionary condition for the middle class; it was the claim by the disinherited of the great revolution that they, too, had rights, and so announced the class struggle between capitalists and proletarians.

Social conflict broke the unity of "the people" within the nation; national conflicts broke the unity of "the people" throughout Europe. The French Revolution had preached nationalism; it meant by this only the right of existing nations to succeed to the inheritance of their kings. The revolution of 1848 aspired to destroy existing States and to create new ones in accordance with the national principle. This doctrine was destructive of existing monarchies; it menaced also the preponderance of France, the existing Great Power. The "historic nations," Italy, Hungary and Poland, announced their claims in 1848; they were overshadowed by Germany, where the revolutionary idea reached its highest point. The German movement was at once the most romantic and the most radical; and 1848 ushered in "the German century," which has left Europe torn in pieces.

The "historic nations" all had a past, a literature and an intellectual class; their appearance was expected. The surprise of 1848 was the appearance of the "unhistoric nations," the submerged Slav peoples of east-central Europe. Emancipation of the peasants brought to life nations without aristocrats or burghers—their only spokesmen the educated sons of peasants —and therefore at one bound most under the leadership of ideologues. The historic nations, challenging the traditional order of Europe, were themselves challenged by the unhistoric nations. Slovenes and Croats disputed the historic claims of national Italy; Slovenes, Croats, Serbs and Rumanians (not a Slav people, but with similar social conditions) repudiated Great Hungary; the Czechs questioned German predominance in Bohemia; the Poles fought in both camps—they resisted the claims of the Germans in Posnania, yet to the east their own "historic" claims were challenged by the Little Russians or Ukrainians. In the words of Professor Namier: "With 1848 starts the Great European War of every nation against its neighbours." Metternich's Europe, in spite of its dullness, lasted more than a generation; the Europe of Lamartine never came into existence.

The sovereignty of the people was the cardinal doctrine of 1848; all frontiers were to be redrawn and all political institutions remade in its name. Hence the great practical expression of 1848 was direct universal suffrage, practised for the first time: the people were not to be limited in their sovereignty, nor was the power of the people to be weakened by any intermediary. France set the example for the political events of the following hundred years. The sovereign people were offered the "ideologues"; they chose Louis Napoleon. Proudhon, a democrat without illusions, drew the lesson: "Universal suffrage is counter-revolution." This lesson was applied by Bismarck and, later, by Hitler and Mussolini. Hitler, incorporating the General Will of the German people, united Nationalism and Socialism and redrew the map of Europe according to the German principles of 1848. Like the German Radicals of 1848, Hitler ran against the rock of Slav resistance; and the Slav peoples were the residuary legatees of 1848.

(2) *The French Revolution*

February 24, 1848, was the last day of great France, the last
day of the France which had overshadowed the rest of Europe
and had called the tune in political ideas. It was the last time
when France sneezed and the rest of Europe caught a cold;
henceforth France caught colds from others, as in the recent
malady of Vichy. In 1848 the radicals of all Europe still
looked to Paris, as the Communists now look to Moscow.
Paris was the mother of revolutions; but in 1848 her progeny
got out of control. Though there had been previous outbreaks
in Galicia and in Sicily the revolution in Paris gave the signal
for the real storm, and the street fighting which overthrew
Louis Philippe brought down, too, Metternich and the
absolute monarchy in Prussia. Yet the revolutions which swept
Europe did not remain under the spell of French ideas; still
less did they restore French hegemony in Europe, as the
French Radicals had expected. Instead the French began to
realize that the victory of the national principle, which they
had launched, far from restoring Napoleon's domination
of Europe, would destroy French security and would bring
France under the threatening shadow of a Germany more
powerful than herself.

Once a revolution is successful the revolutionaries become
conservative in their turn. This is the key to French history
in the hundred and fifty years since the Great Revolution.
In 1789 the rights of man were subversive of the existing
order and had to oe fought for; later they became the existing
order and had to be defended, until to-day the adherents of
the rights of man are the most conservative element in
European politics. The transition from one attitude to the
other took place in France between February and June,
1848; on both occasions the radicals fought—but on different
sides of the barricades. The revolution of February 24 had
no deep-seated cause; as Proudhon said, it was made "without
an idea." The demand for an extension of the franchise, which
was its excuse, could have been met without a revolution;
indeed, Louis Philippe had already granted it before his fall.
But peaceful reform would have seemed a drab outcome,

unworthy of the traditions of revolutionary France. The revolution was, in fact, its own object; the emotional experience provided the satisfaction of a religious conversion. A Radical journalist expressed this: "My hopes are in an act of providence, in a religious transformation to regenerate society." The revolutionaries repeated the attitudes of 1789, as in 1939 the French tried, in vain, to recapture the inspiration of 1914. Tocqueville, sitting in the Chamber when it was invaded by the mob, was puzzled that he felt no fear; suddenly he realized that he was watching men striking postures which they had seen in an old print, not a spontaneous revolution—it is difficult to be frightened of a musket which was loaded sixty years before and has become a theatrical prop.

The radicals established a Provisional Government; this was hard put to it to find a programme. Lamartine describes the members of the Provisional Government sitting round and racking their heads in vain for some great symbolical act which should make the revolution worth while. He solved the problem by proposing the abolition of the death penalty; within four months it was restored for political offences and applied wholesale to those who had won the battle of February for the Provisional Government. Though the radicals proclaimed the sovereignty of the people, they feared it in practice. They had no agrarian programme with which to win the allegiance of the peasants, who made up the majority of the population. The revolution of 1789 gave the peasants their land, free of feudal duties; the revolution of 1848 compelled the peasants to pay their debts and increased the taxation on land. For the Radicals of 1848 tried to combine revolution and a stable currency; not surprisingly, the peasants preferred Louis Napoleon, distinguished by his debts as well as by his great name. The radicals knew that universal suffrage would go against them; yet they insisted on perishing from their own principles. Lamartine declared: "The people must be left free to make mistakes." This mistake was the Second Empire.

Before 1848 the radicals had thought little of internal affairs. Their greatest grievance had been against the humiliation of the Congress of Vienna, and they expected to escape from their problems by renewing the glories of revolutionary war. Lamartine reserved his highest rhetoric for the circular dispatch in which he declared that France no longer recognized the treaties of 1815. Still, though France wished to see these treaties disappear, she would not herself make the effort to destroy them. Besides, on reflection it was not in the interests of France to replace the weak States across the Alps and the Rhine by a united Italy and a united Germany; and—in spite of past lip-service to the idea—even Radical Frenchmen saw the defeat of Italian and German nationalism with some relief. The army originally prepared to go to the assistance of revolutionary Italy went off in 1849 to restore the Pope. There could be no such practical arguments against aiding Poland, and war for Poland was the slogan with which the extreme radicals, Blanqui and Barbès, attempted to overthrow the Provisional Government on May 15. In 1848, as in 1939, France could aid Poland only by resuming the mastery of Europe which Napoleon had won and then lost; the task was already beyond her. Hence the defeat of Blanqui and his associates marked the turning-point in France's position in the world, as well as being the crisis of the revolution.

Still, behind the revolutionary echoes a true revolution existed. This was the movement of the town working-classes, especially in Paris. The Great Revolution had found no place for them; rather it had established an alliance of peasants and *bourgeoisie* against them. Now to the traditional rights of man they claimed to add "the right to work." This demand sprang from handicraft workers, threatened by the machine, not from factory workers, enslaved to it. In England at the same time the workers, more mature, were demanding the right to work less. "The right to work" was a demand for recognition rather than an economic programme; it was rejected by all those who had profited by the Great Revolution. The result was the June Days, the most formidable slave-war of modern times. The workers of Paris fought without leaders and without hope against a united front of nobles, middle class and peasants. Reactionaries and radicals, estranged since the execution of Louis XVI, were reconciled over the

bodies of the Parisian workers. The June Days showed that
radicalism would not satisfy the working-class; they became,
and remained, an alien body in the French Republic. The
radicals of 1848 had tried to be a "third force"; instead the
June Days drove France into the arms of Napoleon. A hundred
years later, the shadow of the June Days, and of its sequel,
still lies across French political life.

(3) *Vienna and Berlin*

On March 13, 1848, revolution reached Vienna: Metternich
was driven from power after thirty-nine years of office. The
Vienna revolution was the central event of 1848, as significant
as the fall of the Bastille in 1789. The Bastille was an antiquated
fortress, virtually without a garrison; Metternich a feeble old
man without supporters. Yet both symbolized the old order
and brought it down with them. Monarchical authority over
"subjects" lost its divine sanction on July 14, 1789; dynastic
rights over peoples lost its hold on March 13, 1848. The
Rights of Man triumphed in the streets of Paris; the rights
of nations in the streets of Vienna. It was the end of government based on tradition. Henceforth peoples could be ruled
only by consent—or by force. European history of the following hundred years recounts the oscillations between these
two methods.

Though the Habsburg dynasty maintained a precarious
existence in 1848 (and indeed for another seventy years) the
fall of Metternich ended its independent position. Previously
it had stood above the peoples; thereafter it manœuvred
between them. The Vienna revolution was the cardinal date
in the history of both national Hungary and national Italy;
it was a victory for Kossuth and Mazzini. National Italy
sought only separation from Central Europe (a separation
never fully achieved from the days of the Triple Alliance
to the Axis or the present). National Hungary hoped to remain
a great State without the Habsburgs, or rather to substitute
the Magyar landowners for the dynasty as the ruling authority
in Central Europe. This aim was subsequently realized,
though in association with the dynasty, in the period of

Dualism (1867–1918); in the end it brought "thousand-year-old" Hungary to ruin.

Once the dynasty lost its traditional appeal, Central Europe needed some other principle of association. The Slav peoples (who were in the majority) would not accept German and Magyar hegemony which was offered them as an alternative. Against this they raised the demand for their own national freedom and thus prepared the way for the national States of 1918. Still, they wished also for association; and the few far-sighted Habsburg ministers, after Metternich's fall, saw that the Empire could be saved only by invoking the peasant masses against the disruptive Liberalism and Nationalism of the middle classes. This was the significance of the emancipation of the peasants on September 7, 1848, the enduring achievement of the Austrian revolution. Aristocrats and liberals alike accused the Habsburg ministers of "Communism." A century later the same programme is being operated, though by the heirs of the Romanovs, not of the Habsburgs.

Still, the Vienna revolution found its greatest immediate impact in Germany. National Germany, too, was born in the streets of Vienna. If Hungary and Italy were to shake off the Habsburgs the remaining Austrian dominions could also follow the national principle: the way seemed open for Greater Germany. This faced the Hohenzollerns, the only other real power in Germany, with a problem of existence. If they resisted German nationalism they would be swept aside; if they went with it they would be submerged. Frederick William IV, astute though neurotic, avoided the dilemma and, with unconscious genius, stumbled on the programme of Little Germany. The revolution of March 18, 1848, in Berlin, though a victory for liberalism, did not break Hohenzollern power; the Army remained confident and intact. Frederick William IV granted a Constitution with a semblance of goodwill; this was his bid for German leadership. He announced: "Prussia merges into Germany." The phrase was fraudulent. Prussia continued to exist with an independent strength; the German liberals were invited to accept Berlin as the capital of Germany, solely in virtue of Frederick

William's word. The revolutions in Vienna and Berlin offered to Germany alternative solutions. The Vienna revolution aspired to a Greater Germany, based on radical violence, which would embrace all Germans and extend German supremacy throughout south-eastern Europe. The Berlin revolution was the first announcement of a more limited Germany, based on an alliance of moderate liberalism and Prussian military strength, and which would repudiate the German inheritance in the south-east. Berlin anticipated Bismarck, and Vienna Hitler.

In 1848 neither programme won unreserved acceptance. National Germany rejected both Vienna and Berlin, the two seats of power; it looked to Frankfurt, symbol of unification by consent. The greatest event in the history of German liberalism was the meeting of the National Assembly at Frankfurt on May 18, 1848. The Frankfurt Parliament hoped to give Germany freedom and unity; but above these it rated power (Macht). When German claims were challenged in Bohemia and in Posen, German liberals forgot the Rights of Man and invoked the right of the stronger; they expected the Austrian and Prussian armies to provide the strength which they themselves did not possess. They applauded the Habsburg victory in Prague over the Czechs and sought to use Prussian power against the Poles. In November the Frankfurt liberals even welcomed the victory of Frederick William IV over the Prussian Parliament, which they regarded as an impudent rival.

These victories did not help liberal Germany; it became the next victim of the power which it worshipped. In April, 1849, delegates from Frankfurt went humbly to Berlin to offer the Imperial Crown to Frederick William IV: liberal Germany was willing to merge into Prussia. The offer was rejected by Frederick William IV, and the Frankfurt Parliament was soon after dispersed by Prussian soldiers. Nevertheless Bismarck took up the offer, on terms still more favourable to Prussia, twenty years later.

Two great negatives were the legacy of the German revolutions of 1848. Dynastic power could not survive unless it took on a national colouring; on the other hand the Germans could not maintain the hegemony over Poles and Czechs on which the liberals most of all insisted unless they compromised with the possessors of power. This compromise is still sought by the Germans a century later; equally the foreign Powers who have replaced the dynasties compete for the favour of German nationalism.

March 13 will not be celebrated this year in Germany; it is the symbol of Greater Germany and so of Hitler's vanished Empire. The Russians have decreed March 18 as Germany's "day of freedom": like Frederick William IV they hope to pass off a spurious revolution as the real thing and, succeeding the Hohenzollerns as rulers in Berlin, announce that Prussia merges into Germany. As in the days of Bismarck, Little Germany is the best outcome for the Russians—a protection at once against Greater German power and against the West. The Western Powers follow in the footsteps of the Liberals of 1848 to Frankfurt; they, too, will find themselves embarrassed by frontier disputes with Poland and by the agitation of Germans from Bohemia. Disappointment awaits those who seek national Germany at Frankfurt; as in 1848, Frankfurt is the symbol of the Germany of the idea, peaceful, liberal, contented—and non-existent.

(4) *The Slav Congress*

The Slav Congress which met in Prague on June 2, 1848, was the least expected event in the year of revolutions. The Slav peoples of Central Europe had not been allowed for in radical calculations. Engels wrote of the Czechs and Croats (he was unaware even of the existence of the Slovaks): "The natural and inevitable fate of these dying nations was to allow the process of dissolution and absorption by their stronger neighbours [Germany and Hungary] to complete itself." Exception was made only for the Poles, as an historic nation, not as Slavs; the German radicals proposed to push Poland against Russia and then to jettison her later (the reverse of Russia's Polish policy a century later). Since Bohemia had been included in the Holy Roman Empire, it was assumed that it would become part of the new national Germany, and distinguished Bohemians were invited to join the preliminary meetings at Frankfurt. Palacky, the first historian of Bohemia and the recreator of Czech national consciousness, refused the invitation; he repudiated allegiance to Germany—"I am a Bohemian of Slav race"—and looked instead to the Habsburg dynasty as the protector of the Slav peoples from German tyranny. "If the Austrian Empire did not exist, it would have to be created in the interest of Europe and of humanity." This famous sentence launched the programme of Austroslavism, the idea of maintaining a modest national existence under the wing of the most clerical and traditional dynasty in Europe.

In 1848 the dynasty seemed too shaken to act as the sole bond of union between different peoples, and those who feared incorporation in Greater Germany sought some more popular alternative. They thought to have found it in their Slav race. This was more than crude racialism: it assumed that all peoples with a Slav language had a common cultural background. In reality most Slav peoples outside Russia had been submerged by the culture of their conquerors, German, Hungarian, or even Turkish; hence the importance of ethnography in the Slav movement—the evidence for a common Slav "folk" had to be found in the designs on peasant costume or pottery. The Slav Congress was intended as a gesture against the German National Assembly at Frankfurt. This threatened directly only the Czechs and the Slovenes —another reason for draping Slav "folkdom" round the practical political issue. The Slavs of Hungary (Croats, Serbs and Slovaks) were indifferent to the German menace; the Czechs wished to avoid a conflict with Hungary, yet would not repudiate the Slovaks, who alone could swell their numbers.

The real stumbling-block for a common Slav policy came from the Poles. The Poles of Galicia were indisputably Slavs and indisputably Habsburg subjects; yet Russia was their only enemy, and they welcomed both Greater Germany and Great Hungary. The Poles, who were threatened by the Germans, were under Prussian rule in Posnania. To exclude them would weaken the struggle against Frankfurt decisively;

to include them would trespass beyond the frontiers of the Habsburg monarchy and so make nonsense of Austroslavism. In fact, the Slav Congress had stumbled on the Polish problem. The Poles of the Austrian Empire would not work with the Czechs nor against the Germans; the Poles of Posnania would work against the Germans, but equally emphatically would not work with Russia. The Czechs insisted that Poles from outside the Austrian Empire should attend the Congress only as guests; the Poles would not recognize the frontiers of the Polish partitions, and when the Polish section of the Congress met it made the Poles from Posnania full members, one of them, indeed, becoming its chairman.

This intrusion of non-Austrian Slavs had a further embarrassing consequence. No one minded the presence of Serbs from Turkey: the solidarity of the "master nations" did not yet extend to the Turks. But if the Slav Congress was to include all Slavs it was impossible to exclude the greatest branch of the Slav race, and the revolutionary Bakunin imposed himself upon the congress as the solitary, self-appointed representative of the Russian people. Bakunin had no patience with the cautious Austroslavism of Palacky; he demanded both the destruction of the Habsburg Empire and revolution in Russia. His goal was a federation of free peoples, based on the natural democracy of the Slav peasants. Like later versions of Pan-Slavism, Bakunin's vision rested on the dogma of virtues innate in Slav peoples which would save them from the failings of others.

Pan-Slavism evoked no response from the Slav Congress; indeed, Pan-Slavism had sense only as a translation into racial mysticism of the Byzantine and Orthodox heritage shared by some Slav peoples, and almost all those present at Prague were Western and Roman Catholic. The Slav Congress produced two contradictory programmes. The Poles drafted a manifesto to the Peoples of Europe which recognized the existence only of the "historic nations"—Poland, Germany, Hungary and Turkey—and politely invited these to treat their minorities better. The Czechs drafted an address to the Austrian Emperor which asked for the remodelling of the Austrian Empire into a federation based on national units.

Perhaps the most concrete effect of the Congress was its division into three sections—Polish-Ukrainian, Czechoslovak and South Slav—for these anticipated the "national amalgamations" which served as the basis for pseudo-national States (Poland, Czechoslovakia and Yugoslavia) in 1918.

All these programmes received only preliminary statement. The Congress met for the last time on June 12. Then fighting broke out between the Prague radicals, both Czech and German, and the Imperial forces; and on the suppression of the rebellion the Congress was dissolved. In its ten days of activity it had stated all the solutions for the problem of Central Europe which have been attempted from then until now. The Czechs followed Austroslavism for half a century after 1848; its essential condition, a federation of free nationalities, was granted by the Habsburg Emperor only on October 16, 1918, when the Empire was already in ruins. The last echo of Austroslavism was heard in the Slovakia of Tiso and the Croatia of Pavelic. The Poles tried to act as the partners of Greater Germany and Great Hungary in the days of Colonel Beck, and thought that they had reached their aim when they established a common frontier with Hungary in March 1939—six months before their destruction. Bakunin's first demand was fulfilled with the dissolution of the Habsburg monarchy in 1918; failing the establishment of democracy in Russia, the Slavs had to look for support from the Western democracies and suffered ineffaceable disappointment at the time of Munich. Now fear of Germany makes them pretend that Bakunin's second condition has been fulfilled, and the "democracies of the new type" rest on the double pretence of Russian democracy and Slav solidarity.

IV

1848: OPENING OF AN ERA

ROBERT OWEN, on a visit to Paris, described his economic system as "the railway which will take mankind to universal happiness." His phrase crystallized the spirit of the year of revolutions. Movement, and a conviction that Utopia could be reached, were the essence of 1848: underlying these was a faith in the limitless goodness of human nature. The revolutionary cry, "All change!" sounded across Europe. Hope lit the dawn of a new Europe; and mankind clambered into the trains of political and social upheaval, all of which claimed to be directed to the same terminus—the Kingdom of Heaven on Earth. New faiths, new nations, new classes announced their arrival; each was the confident possessor of an exclusive truth. Before 1848 the rights of individuals and of States were a matter of history and of settled law; the revolutions substituted the rule of abstract principle. Louis Phillipe said bitterly of the revolution of 1830 which brought him to the throne: "What perished in France in 1830 was not respect for a dynasty, but respect for anything." This was demonstrated anew in France in 1848 and, for the first time, was demonstrated throughout Europe as well. Reason took the place of respect; and self-interest the place of tradition.

Movement was both the cause of the revolutions and their outcome: the revolutions threw down established landmarks that were already ruinous. In the preceding fifty years tumultuous development had taken the place of imperceptible change. There was an unprecedented growth of population, an unprecedented advance in the methods of industry and of transport, and an unprecedented novelty in the world of ideas; the three together composed the background to the revolutions. The old order had assumed stable populations; these ensured stability between classes and stability between States. For half a century before 1848 the increase of population had been gathering strength, and this contributed more than anything else to the illusion of progress. The increase was less in France than elsewhere in Europe; and the wise student of population figures might already guess that France, hitherto the greatest European Power and the most revolutionary nation, would soon become the most conservative and the least great of the Powers. The universal growth of population had profound consequences. Where the peasant was already free, as in western Germany, the surplus was being pushed into the towns. In the Austrian Empire the peasants could no longer tolerate the burden of feudal dues and of feudal subordination; moreover, with the increasing demand for food, the great landowners could no longer operate their estates by the traditional methods. Both lords and peasants turned against the old order of settled obligations; both demanded freedom of movement and the rule of the market. Almost the first act of the liberal parliament in Hungary was to abolish the old agrarian social order; and the Austrian Constituent Assembly followed suit (its only effective act) on September 7. The destinies of fifty million people were affected. The more prosperous peasants got the chance of survival; the poorer peasants lost their last traditional protection and were the victims both of the richer peasants and of the capitalistic great estates. The way was clear for the emigration to the towns and overseas which characterized the second half of the century. It was no accident that England and Russia, the only countries of Europe to escape the revolutions, had already found the way of emigration before 1848: the road to Siberia had been open since the beginning of the century, and the emigrant-steamers took the life out of Chartism when they began to sail from Liverpool in 1844. The rest of Europe had lacked the technical and social conditions for mass emigration: peasant emancipation came in 1848, and railways followed. These provided a safety valve which postponed further European explosions until the twentieth century. Modern industrial America, as well as modern industrial Europe, would have been impossible without the revolutions of 1848.

The idea of 1848 spread later to Russia; and the Russian

revolutions of the twentieth century were in the true spirit of 1848. In fact, Russia, missing the disillusionment which followed the failure of 1848, alone retained faith in the revolutionary course. America was already democratic, and therefore for her, though there was no need for revolution, there was no need for disillusionment either. For a generation after 1848, and even longer, America offered to the peoples of Europe the economic and political prizes which failure had denied them in Europe. Still, 1848 left no tradition in either Russia or America. Eighteen forty-nine has some meaning in the history of both countries. For Russia it brought a victorious repression of revolution in Hungary; for America it marked the discovery of gold in California. To the present day, the one Great Power offers Europe repression, the other material wealth. Neither can offer the liberty of spirit which was the true aim of 1848.

The staggering growth of towns throughout Europe was a consequence of the revolutions. Still, even before 1848, the swelling towns amazed and alarmed contemporaries; and their isolation—urban islands in a rural continent—emphasized their revolutionary character. The conscious revolutions of 1848 were all exclusively urban. "The German revolution" is a misleading generalization for the Berlin revolution and the Vienna revolution; "the Italian revolution" still more misleading as a title for the revolutions in Venice, Milan, Florence, Rome, Naples and many more. The contrast was sharpest in France. The great revolution of 1789 had been the movement of a people, the revolution of 1848 was a movement of Paris against the rest of the nation. Isolated in place, the revolutions were equally insular in idea: they had no agrarian programme and offered the peasants—troglodytes, in Marx's phrase—nothing but extinction. For the first time news of a revolution passed from one town to another by telegraph; it no longer needed to filter through, and so to affect, the countryside. The revolutionaries travelled by train from one revolution to the next; they had neither eyes nor thoughts for the country through which they passed. The revolutionaries equated revolutions with street-fighting. Their occasional forays into the countryside—from Hecker's raid on Baden in April 1848 to Garibaldi's march across Italy in July 1849—were the organized hikes of town dwellers.

Even the largest towns lacked industrial development. Labour had arrived before capital was ready for it. Only Belgium had experienced an industrial revolution; and therefore, despite its urban character, enjoyed an unique freedom from revolutionary danger. The revolutions elsewhere were not revolts against the machine; they were demands to be employed by it. The slogan of "the right to work" was a symbol of immaturity; an industrial proletariat would have demanded the right to work less—as indeed the English working-class had already done with success in 1847. "The right to work" was a protest as much against social inequality as against harsh living condition. Nevertheless, by formulating this protest in economic terms, it launched the idea that liberty and political equality were negligible, or indeed valueless, in comparison with food and clothing. This idea was not intended by the social revolutionaries of 1848, who took up economic grievances principally in order to add greater force to their political demands. All the same the damage had been done. Continental Socialism, which had its origins in 1848, wrote off political democracy as *bourgeois* and accepted the doctrine that violence and intolerance were a small price to pay for social change. Class war took the place of the struggle for political liberty, and the Rights of Man were a casualty of "the right to work."

The announcement of an economic programme was certainly the startling novelty of 1848; nevertheless the revolutions were not simply the product of economic circumstances. These determined the moment of revolution, not that it should occur. The economic upheaval and the upheaval in men's minds were two aspects of the same process. Certainly the age of coal and iron enforced daring political schemes and made them possible; but equally it needed a daring mind to think of the railway and the blast furnace. The great towns of modern Europe could not have been maintained without railways, steam power and a revolution in agriculture; but the movement to the towns depended just as much on the spread of new ideas which prised men away from their traditional beliefs and traditional surroundings. The railways found people ready to move; otherwise they would have run empty. Reason was the great dissolvent force. This made men dissatisfied with their traditional homes and with their traditional place in society just as much as with the traditional methods of production. The radicals of 1848 were the heirs of eighteenth-century enlightenment: sublimely confident in human nature (except that of their fellow revolutionaries), they believed that their only task was to shake off the hold of established beliefs and established institutions. Their common programme was "to strangle the last king with the bowels of the last priest." The natural goodness of man would do the rest.

The old order, thus dramatically threatened, claimed to depend on habit, on history and on established rights. No historical conflict is, in fact, fought on these easy terms. The old order was itself more rational and artificial—just as the revolutionaries were more traditional—than either side liked to admit. Revolutionary ideas had affected the upper classes before they spread to the masses; and the impact of the great French revolution had long shaken the foundations of the European system. Men were argued into conservatism as they were argued into revolution. The kings who were threatened by the movements of 1848 had less than a century of possession behind them, and many more were the creations of Napoleon. Even the house of Habsburg, the only genuine historic dynasty, had acquired a new title and new territories a generation previously and had knocked all life out of historic institutions everywhere in its dominions except in Hungary —and there from lack of strength, not of will. The "old aristocracy" was a creation of the eighteenth, or occasionally of the seventeenth century. Most of all the territorial settlement of the Congress of Vienna was as artificial as the Empire of Napoleon which it replaced. The peace which followed the Napoleonic wars sprang from exhaustion, not from belief or from content; and the society which perished in 1848 had no moral justification other than the desire of the possessing classes to enjoy their privileges.

The kings, aristocrats and states of the Vienna system had not even given themselves the trouble of being born; they had been conjured up ready-made by conservative theorists. Thus Metternich, to give historic character to the Austrian Empire (which had acquired legal existence only in 1804), proposed to invent for the Emperor a traditional ceremony of coronation. Metternich, symbol and chief exponent of Conservatism, claimed to be building a dam against revolution. In reality, his effort to set up a universal "system" of political ideas and institutions was typical of an eighteenth-century doctrinaire. He approached politics in the spirit of Robespierre: the only difference was in his employer. The dissolvent of reason could have been resisted only by communities with a living history; few such existed on the continent of Europe, and these few (Switzerland, Hungary and perhaps the Low Countries) did not accord with Metternich's conservatism. As a result, the system of Metternich was not overthrown in 1848; it collapsed. This collapse astonished contemporaries, other than Metternich himself: he had always appreciated the artificiality of his own system and had never felt the faith which he demanded in others.

In 1848 Europe broke consciously with its past. This was the indelible achievement ·of the year of revolutions. Yet more than destruction was intended. Bakunin, most extreme representative of the spirit of revolution, once declared that if his plans succeeded he would at once begin to pull down again everything he had ever made; this did not take the zest from a lifetime of planning. The radicals of all schools were as convinced as Metternich of the need for belief; and, unlike Metternich, themselves believed in the systems which they expounded. Their systems, too, were universal and dogmatic. All assumed that reason was adequate as the sole guide in human affairs; and they assumed also that there was no limit to what reason could do. The revolutionaries differed as to the means by which the human race might be made perfect; none disputed that the goal would be attained. The radical systems provided new Absolutes for old and gave final answers in politics, in society and in international affairs. The sovereignty of the people overthrew the sovereignty of kings; nations took the place of states; and intellect ousted heredity as the source of authority.

Though the sovereignty of the people had already served as inspiration to the French revolution of 1789, its operation had been restricted. The distinguishing mark of 1789 had been the confidence that universal principles could be limited in their application and a revolution arrested in its course. This expectation was not proved false until 1848. When all hereditary rights were repudiated, the right of private property had remained inviolate and was indeed reinforced; and the dogma of the sovereignty of the people was used to justify the franchise of the property-owning middle class. In 1848 the term of this compromise expired; and the *bourgeoisie*, once the leaders of revolution, became the symbol of conservatism. Almost the first act of the victorious revolution in France was to abolish the property qualification and to proclaim universal suffrage. This became everywhere the most concrete expression of the revolutionary programme. Only Hungary, which combined—or perhaps stifled—revolutionary principle with historic institutions, held out against universal suffrage until the twentieth century. The events of 1848 challenged also the economic privilege of the owners of property. The June Days in Paris gave dramatic announcement of the arrival of a new revolutionary class, "the proletariat." The June rising was not fought to promote any practical economic change; it was a social war, a slave revolt, and its repudiation of the moral superiority of the *bourgeoisie* could not be wiped out by all the executions and deportations which followed defeat. Before the June Days private property had been regarded as essential for liberty; after the June Days it became the symbol of oppression, and the capitalist took the place of priest and noble as the object of democratic hostility. Henceforth the *bourgeoisie* was morally on the defensive, ashamed and anxious. This was true not only of the French *bourgeoisie*, who had genuinely experienced the "social peril." The alarm of the June Days spread across Europe; indeed, apprehension increased as the reality of danger became more remote. The middle classes outside France abandoned the revolutionary cause almost before they had taken it up and sought for allies against a proletariat which was still imaginary. Thus, the October Revolution in Vienna, though it had a programme with no social implications, sent the German-Austrian middle classes over to the side of absolutism; and within a few years of 1848 German liberalism came to regard universal suffrage as its mortal enemy. The French *bourgeoisie* had pride enough to remain radical though they ceased to be revolutionary and adhered to the sovereignty of the people in the sense that they took into partnership the French peasants who had saved them in the June Days. Though universal suffrage, the work of the revolution of 1848, became everywhere a mainstay of conservatism, in France it sustained at least the Third Republic and later, in the Dreyfus case, upheld the Rights of Man. In Germany, however, it was the instrument of Bismarck and in Austria it became in 1907 the last prop of the Empire of Francis Joseph.

In the world of nations, too, the revolutions of 1848 ended the compromise which had been the outcome of the revolution of 1789. The French revolutionaries had launched the national principle; they supposed that this would operate to the sole advantage of France and that when all else of the old order was destroyed the predominance of France would remain unchallenged. France liberated other nations as the French *bourgeoisie* liberated the French people: freed from their hereditary rulers, they were expected to welcome French leadership instead. The Empire of Napoleon expressed the French version of the national principle: German, Italian, Polish and even South Slav nationalism were evoked as auxiliary weapons for the French cause. France was the only one who knew how to wield the national appeal, and remained the greatest single power in Europe even after the fall of Napoleon; the other Great Powers of the Continent were states, not nations, and therefore without the strength of popular enthusiasm. Thus the French nation claimed the cultural and political heritage of Louis XIV, despite the guillotining of Louis XVI and the renewed expulsion of the Bourbons in July 1830. This cultural headship was recognized for the last time at the beginning of 1848, when the other nations of Europe waited for the February Revolution in Paris before starting their own. Thereafter it was no longer enough to have taken the trouble to be born French. The laws of inheritance were repudiated between nations as much as between individuals. The lesson was not lost on the French themselves; henceforth the French nation was as much imperilled as, say, the dynasty of Habsburg by European upheavals, and France—previously the promoter of change—became the principal advocate of conservatism and of the *status quo*.

In 1848 every nation followed the example set by the French in 1789. Each claimed to be perfect: each, therefore, was entitled to lay down its own limits or, if it preferred, to recognize none. Moreover, each nation asserted a purity and greatness of character which made it an example to Europe and justified its bringing other less noble people under its own rule. Thus, Poland had long announced herself as "the Christ among the nations," and her liberation was regarded as the first object of the revolutionary cause; this liberation did not, however, extend to the Ukrainians under Polish rule. Similarly Mazzini, despite his denunciations of French arrogance, set up Italy as "God's word in the midst of the nations." Rome was to be the capital of a new federation of nations, all duly humble, which were to be cut and shaped to suit Italy's convenience. Kossuth, too, insisted on the unique civilization and political gifts of the Magyars. Though partly Slovak by birth, he denied the existence of a Slovak nation, and, since he could not deny the existence of the Serbs, proposed to root them out with the sword.

Magyar exclusiveness was relatively harmless, except to the subject nations of Hungary. The will to dominate was a more dangerous matter when it was taken up by the Germans, already the most numerous nationality in Europe. The revolutions of 1848 discovered "the German mission." This mission was simple: it was, simply, to be German. Europe was corrupt —French sophistication, English materialism, outworn institutions were all to be redeemed by the irruption of the clear-eyed, healthy German barbarian:

> *Und es soll am Deutschen Wesen*
> *Noch einmal die Welt genesen.*

A unique character was found in the German spirit (*Deutscher Geist*), and for that matter even in German rivers and trees—the one wetter and the other more arboreal than any others. Other nations based their claims on superiority of culture, as in the case of France or Italy, or at any rate on superiority of class—as Polish and Magyar nationalism sprang from their landed nobility. German nationalism was the first to depend solely on language: the future Germany was to extend wherever German was spoken. The *Volksdeutsche* were an invention of 1848. Since Germany had no "natural frontiers"—or none that gave such an easy excuse for expansion as the Rhine to France or the Alps to Italy—national Germany used a simpler argument and claimed whatever was necessary to her existence. Thus Bohemia, despite its Czech majority, could, according to Engels, "only exist henceforth as a part of Germany"; and the German liberal spokesman at Frankfurt said of western Poland: "Our right is that of the stronger, the right of conquest." This phrase supplied the basic theme of German history, until it turned against Germany a century later.

Resistance to German claims was not delayed until the twentieth century; it was the motive of the Slav Congress which met at Prague on June 2, 1848. The Slav peoples of eastern Europe were individually too small to hold out against German pressure; therefore, improving on the German model which had made language the basis of nationality, they tried to find a bond of alliance in ethnography and philology. The Slav Congress had practical motives of defence against German nationalism and had no time to trouble about the virtues of the Slav character. Still, even at Prague, Bakunin, one of the inventors of Slav solidarity, found in the Slavs "an amazing freshness and incomparably more natural intelligence and energy than in the Germans"; and he expected them "to renew the decadent Western world." The Slavs of the Austrian and Turkish Empires had enough to do renewing themselves and thereafter quarrelling with each other. The only contribution Russia made to the Western world in 1848–49 was to crush the revolution in Hungary. But the spirit of radicalism was not permanently arrested at the Russian frontier; and Pan-Slavism, which evoked little response outside Russia, became the delayed gift of 1848 to the Russian intellectuals. In the twentieth century they escaped from this ethnic intolerance only with the aid of class intolerance, which was the other legacy of 1848 to mankind.

The revolutions of 1848 dispelled the Utopian dreams of the eighteenth-century rationalists. These had supposed that mankind would attain universal happiness if traditional beliefs were abandoned and traditional authorities overthrown. The experiences after 1789 did not destroy this idea. Social concord accompanied the rule of the *bourgeoisie*, and a true international order was established with the Empire of Napoleon; it could plausibly be argued that achievement fell short of the ideal only because success was incomplete. Had the tricolour really "toured the world," universal happiness could have been expected to follow. In 1848 no bounds were drawn against revolutionary victory: no European country, except Belgium, escaped, and the established system lost its traditional authority for ever. The outcome was conflict, not concord. The June Days announced class war; the record of the German, Italian and Hungarian revolutions announced war between nations. Peaceful agreement and government by consent are possible only on the basis of ideas common to all parties; and these ideas must spring from habit and from history. Once reason is introduced, every man, every class, every nation becomes a law unto itself; and the only right which reason understands is the right of the stronger. Reason formulates universal principles and is therefore intolerant: there can be only one rational society, one rational nation, ultimately one rational man. Decision between rival reasons can be made only by force. This lesson was drawn by the greatest political genius who observed the events of 1848: "The great questions of our day will not be settled by resolutions and majority votes—that was the mistake of the men of 1848 and 1849—but by blood and iron." After 1848, the idea that disputes between classes could be settled by compromise or that discussion was an effective means of international relations was held only in England and America, the two countries which escaped the revolutions.

The liberals, the moderate men, shirked the problem of authority; it was faced by the radicals. They found a substitute for tradition in "the religion of humanity," just as their nationalism took the place of the decayed loyalty to kings. Above all, they found a substitute for the hereditary governing class in themselves. "The aristocracy of intellect" had a limitless confidence in its right to govern; for it spoke "in the name of the people." The radical leaders nominated themselves to this post: none of the great revolutionaries —not Marx nor Engels, Bakunin nor Blanqui—ever secured election by a democratic constituency, and, for the matter of that, none of them was sure of a majority even among the circle of his close associates. The greatest radical effort in France was the demonstration of March 16, which demanded that elections to the Constituent Assembly be postponed until the people were fit to exercise the franchise, that is, until they were willing to vote for the Radical leaders. Blanqui, when asked how long the postponement should be, answered: "For some months, or perhaps years." By democracy the men of 1848 did not mean the rule of the majority; they meant rather the rule of the discontented, a reversal of the previous order of society. The essence of 1848 was belief in movement; therefore only those elements of the population who desired change were democratic. The theoretical justification for this outlook was provided by Marx; it was his great contribution to history. Marx found the motive force of history in economic change; and this force was now impelling mankind from capitalism to socialism. Since movement and democracy were synonymous, only those who desired socialism were "the people." Marx could thus eliminate the peasants from his calculations, though they made up the great majority everywhere in Europe; and democracy could be turned into "the dictatorship of the proletariat." Marx was a man of the Enlightenment. He held that every man would recognize his own interest and follow it; therefore every proletarian would be a socialist. The proposition could be more usefully reversed: anyone who was not a socialist was not a proletarian. But the dictatorship was not really to be exercised even by those working men who accepted the theories of the learned Dr. Marx. The workers were to be led by the communists, "everywhere the most resolute and progressive element of the working class." Since the communists in 1848 consisted of Marx and Engels, this was a satisfactory conclusion—and has proved a satisfactory conclusion for communists ever since. The radical theorists were led inevitably from belief in the people to belief in themselves; and so to advocacy of authoritarian government. Marx was more self-satisfied and despotic than Metternich, the other system-maker from the Rhineland.

Yet these resolute and progressive leaders never displayed their talents in a revolution. The original outbreaks had no recognized leaders; and no one knows the names of the leaders of the June Days in Paris nor of the October Revolution in Vienna. The name of an individual leader in the rising of May 15 in Paris has been preserved; he is thought to have been a police spy. Only Kossuth and Mazzini experienced the practical tasks of revolutionary government; and the experience of Mazzini was not very serious. For the most part the self-styled spokesmen of the people were always trying to catch up on revolutions which had taken them by surprise, as Marx and Engels were still correcting the proofs of their revolutionary programme, the *Communist Manifesto*, when the first barricades were already built and the first shots were being fired. Bakunin distinguished himself by arriving in time for the Dresden revolution of May 1849. This was an accident—he was leaving Dresden for an imaginary revolution elsewhere and was prevented from reaching the railway station by unexpected barricades.

There would have been no revolutions in 1848 if it had depended on the revolutionary leaders. The revolutions made themselves; and the true heroes of 1848 were the masses. The Radical intellectuals had supposed that, once tradition was overthrown, the masses would acknowledge instead the claims of intellect. Nietzsche expressed later this great illusion of 1848: "Dead are all Gods. Now the superman shall live." The masses never responded to the ambitions of the intellectuals. Though the masses, too, sought the superman, they sought in him an extension of themselves. The first of these supermen, concentrating the impulses and contradictions of the masses, was Napoleon III. He was a clever French guess at the future, not the real thing; for France remained too conservative in institutions and social structure to experience the full rule of the masses. The real superman of the masses was Hitler, in whom anonymity was personified; or perhaps even more in the enigmatical *Politbureaus* of the "new democracies," who have put the superman into commission.

In a deeper sense, the true superman, for whom 1848 prepared the way, has turned out to be the masses themselves. The masses have performed labours greater than those of Hercules and have accomplished miracles more wonderful than those of a divine Saviour; more than any individual superman, they have shown themselves to be beyond good and evil. The age which began in 1848 was the age of the masses: the age of mass production, of mass migration and of mass war. In the pursuit of universal happiness everything became universal: universal suffrage, universal education, universal military service, finally universal destruction. The train which Robert Owen signalled has been driven by the masses themselves; the intellectuals have remained passengers, criticizing—or more occasionally—commending the train's progress. The historic task of the intellectuals was to sever mankind from its roots and to launch it on its career of movement. This was the task which was accomplished in 1848.

V

DE TOCQUEVILLE IN 1848

REVOLUTION is for society what a passionate love is for the individual; those who experience it are marked for ever, separated from their own past and from the rest of mankind. Some writers have captured the ecstasy of love; hardly any have rekindled the soul-purging fires of revolution. The writer of genius lives, for the most part, in a private world; it is not surprising that he deals usually with private passions. There have been some good observers of revolution —the best of them, I would guess, John Reed. Still, they observe from outside; it is like reading about the love-affair of the man next door. Two writers of the highest eminence, Lamartine and Trotsky, played the leading part in a revolution and created works of surpassing literary merit, but though their books tell us much about Lamartine and Trotsky, they do not tell us what revolution is like. The more brilliantly they write, the more the truth eludes them. For revolution calls in question the foundations of social life; it can be grasped only by one who has experienced it and yet possesses the detachment of a political psychologist.

Alexis de Tocqueville was this unique man; and his *Recollections of 1848* is the best book about a revolution ever written by a contemporary. Yet even Tocqueville was overwhelmed by his experience. This book is not a finished work, a complete work of art like his two masterpieces, *Democracy in America* and *The "Ancien Régime" and the Revolution*. He wrote to instruct himself, not to persuade the public. Usually he reined in his brilliance; here, writing only for himself, he was not ashamed to be clever. The *Recollections* were only published thirty years after his death and then only with many omissions, where his pen still seemed too sharp or— more occasionally—where his political judgment ran counter to the illusions of the Third Republic.

Alexis de Tocqueville was a liberal aristocrat: he understood both the world that was dying and the world that was coming. As a historian in politics, he both observed events and tried to shape them. Liberty was his passion; and his life was dominated by the question—how can liberty survive the fall of traditional institutions and of traditional morality? Louis Philippe and the men of the *bourgeois* monarchy thought that society could exist without belief: they pinned their faith to legality and supposed that nothing could happen so long as they observed the terms of the Charter. "They resembled the man who refused to believe that his house was on fire, because he had the key to it in his pocket." The Opposition were in no better case; they evoked the spectre of revolution without ever fearing that it would become a reality. Their sole motive was "a taste for holding office and a desire to live on the public money." Tocqueville describes this as "the secret malady which has undermined all former [French] governments and which will undermine all governments to come." Tocqueville was alone in his doubts. A few weeks before the revolution he asked—how can you expect men to respect private property when all other beliefs and privileges have lost their force? The French revolution of 1848 posed "the social question"; it is still without an answer.

Earlier revolutions had been the work of the middle classes; the masses had been merely cannon-fodder. In 1848 the masses acted independently, without leaders and without a programme. This was symbolized on the morning of February 24, when Tocqueville passed along the deserted boulevard:

> There was hardly a soul to be seen, although it was nearly nine o'clock; but . . . the great trees along the curb came tumbling down into the roadway as though of their own accord. These acts of destruction were the work of isolated individuals, who went about their business silently, regularly and hurriedly, preparing in this way the materials for the barricades which others were to erect.

The political events of February 24 had no connection with this elemental force; they merely echoed the sentiments of previous revolutions—the love-affair expressed the nostalgic regrets of a middle-aged man.

Men were fruitlessly endeavouring to warm themselves at the fire of our fathers' passions, imitating their gestures and attitudes as they had seen them represented on the stage, but unable to imitate their enthusiasm or to be inflamed with their fury. . . . Although I clearly saw that the catastrophe of the piece would be a terrible one, I was never able to take the actors very seriously, and the whole seemed to me like a bad tragedy performed by provincial actors.

The leaders did not know what to do with the revolution for which they had become responsible: "in a rebellion, as in a novel, the most difficult part to invent is the end." The only novelty was universal suffrage; this "shook the country from top to bottom without bringing to light a single new man worthy of coming to the front."

Universal suffrage revealed an aspect of the social question which had never occurred to the revolutionaries. "In establishing universal suffrage they thought they were summoning the people to the assistance of the Revolution; they were only giving them arms against it." Alexis de Tocqueville was almost the first to realize that once the peasants acquired their land free of landlords and feudal dues they would become the most conservative of all classes. This was not grasped by Marx or by later Marxists, who went on treating "workers and peasants" as a revolutionary combination until the events of 1932 in the Ukraine and the present political situation in eastern Europe revealed that the conflict between town workers and peasants is the most ghastly as it is the most fierce of all civil wars. In 1848 the revolutionaries, faced with a conservative National Assembly, were at a loss how to proceed. They did not attempt to conquer the countryside, or even to seduce it; they supposed that it would be enough to stage a new revolution in Paris. The last of the romantic revolutions occurred on May 15; its only programme was war for the liberation of Poland. It was then that Tocqueville set eyes on the most persistent of revolutionaries:

He had wan, emaciated cheeks, white lips, a sickly, wicked and repulsive expression, a dirty pallor, the appearance of a mouldy corpse; he wore no visible linen; an old black frock-coat tightly covered his lean, withered limbs; he seemed to have passed his life in a sewer and to have just left it. I was told it was Blanqui.

May 15 brought all the known revolutionaries to prison; and their absence completed the terrible impact of the June Days:

> the most extensive and the most singular insurrection that has occurred in our history and perhaps in any other. . . . The insurgents fought without a war-cry, without leaders, without flags and yet with a marvellous harmony and an amount of military experience that astonished the oldest officers. . . . It was not a political struggle, but a struggle of class against class, a sort of Servile War . . . the revolt of one whole section of the population against another.

The proletariat had appeared on the stage of history; even Marx drew all his teachings of the proletarian revolution from the June Days. Yet Marx saw less deeply than Tocqueville. The revolution of the masses was a revolution of destruction. Marx regarded the proletariat merely as a slave of the lamp, which would carry him to supreme power; Tocqueville recognized that the masses had repudiated all leadership, the leadership of Blanqui and of Barbès as much as the leadership of Lamartine and of Ledru-Rollin. The contrast explains much that happened in his day and more in ours. The Communist revolutions, far from fulfilling the wish of the masses, establish a dictatorship over the masses; they are the last device by which intellectuals bar the way against anarchy. When traditions and beliefs have perished, only force remains; this cannot be concealed by synthetic beliefs and simulated devotions. Yet force cannot provide a lasting answer. One day the masses will knock again at the door—and they will knock more fiercely at the Communist door than at any other.

Tocqueville's revolutionary memories end abruptly with the days of June. The revolution was over. There follows a strange epilogue, out of tone with the rest of the book, yet essential to it—memoirs of the few months when Tocqueville attempted to lead a life of action. Of course he had acted during the revolution. He had been elected a member of the National Assembly, he had kept his courage on May 15 and during the June Days, he had served—though without much effect—on the committee which drafted the Constitution. Still, this was not action of the first order. Twelve months later, in June 1849, Tocqueville suddenly appeared as Foreign

Minister in a cabinet formed "to save the Republic." The great political philosopher proved a signal failure as a practical politician. The lover of liberty became the minister of Louis Napoleon, looking for support to a clericalist majority in the Assembly; and this government of "pure" Republicans first suppressed a radical rising in the streets of Paris and then restored Papal rule in Rome. Had Tocqueville remained longer in power, he would have anticipated the foreign policy of Vichy; for, arguing that France was in decline, he proposed to build up a united Germany as a barrier against Russia. There is some danger in public life from stupid politicians; there is even more from politicians who are too clever. Political understanding of the highest order led Tocqueville into being the associate of Louis Napoleon and of the clericals; it would have been better if he had understood less. He wished to show that Republicans could be conservative in home and foreign policy. This served to suppress the radicals and to destroy the Roman republic; it did not save the republic in France.

Tocqueville knew that somewhere he had gone wrong. When he left office, after some four months, he withdrew for ever from public life; and his apology in this last chapter is laboured, unconvincing even to himself. He had fallen victim to the doctrine of "the lesser evil"—better Louis Napoleon than anarchy, better Falloux and his clerical associates than a new radical revolution. So nowadays we say: better Wall Street than the Kremlin, better de Gaulle than the Communists. Yet Tocqueville himself, in the conclusion of *Democracy in America*, had seen the falsity of this argument; liberty cannot be saved by resistance. He could not apply this teaching when it came to his own country. The social peril threw him off his balance. Hence the malignancy of his picture of Blanqui, who, despite his madness and his pallor (acquired from a lifetime of imprisonment) was also a soldier of liberty—and one who paid a far higher price for it than Tocqueville. No doubt the masses threatened all sorts of "civilized" values; the answer to this danger was to bring the masses within the pale of civilization, not to shoot them down in the June Days. After all, anarchy is a form of liberty, which is more than can be said for dictatorship or clericalism. The greatest invention of 1848, which Tocqueville disowned, was Social Democracy; this was the only way in which civilization could be saved.

Thus Tocqueville's recollections provide an object-lesson as well as a social analysis of the first order. They are a warning against being too clever in politics; in fact, the intellectual more than others should have simple principles and should stick to them. Liberty has to be defended against all comers; all the same, the constant enemies of liberty are on the right, and the lover of liberty must never be shaken from his position on the left. Above all, he who loves liberty must have faith in the people. Otherwise he will, like Tocqueville, withdraw from public life and despair of the future.

VI

FRANCIS JOSEPH: THE LAST AGE OF
THE HABSBURGS

On December 2, 1848, Francis Joseph became Emperor of Austria. He was to reign for almost sixty-eight years, the longest effective reign of modern times. His life spanned the epochs of history. Metternich had ceased to be Imperial Chancellor less than nine months before his accession; two years after his death Austria-Hungary disintegrated into national States. When he was born, Napoleon's son, the King of Rome, was living in Vienna as an Austrian archduke; when he died Adolf Hitler, still an Austrian subject, was serving in the German Army. His reign opened in revolution and closed in war.

Francis Joseph himself fought two wars: in the first he lost his Italian territories; in the second he lost the hegemony of Germany. He started a third war and did not live to see its end; this end was the loss of everything. He won no wars; he lost more territory than he gained. His success was in surviving at all. He was a symbol of rigidity and of resistance, if not of life, in an Imperial organization which, while it had lost creative power, refused to break in pieces. He called himself "the last monarch of the old school" and imagined himself at one with Charles V or Louis XIV. Their pride rested on unquestioning self-confidence; his was always conscious of the challenge of "the revolution." He represented traditional beliefs and institutions, when these had been forced on to the defensive; like them he lacked faith even in himself. He always expected failure and disappointment, and he always got them.

The manner of his accession set the pattern for his reign. The Court was at the little Moravian town of Olomouc, in refuge from the Vienna Revolution of October 1848. The revolution had been crushed, and the counter-revolutionary

Prime Minister, Felix Schwarzenberg, wanted to show by a striking gesture that a new era of ruthless power had opened. The mild, half-witted Emperor Ferdinand was therefore pushed aside in favour of his nephew Francis Joseph, the young pupil of clericalist soldiers. The actual abdication was hurried through in a room of the archbishop's palace before a few Court officials. No one had had time or opportunity to look up the precedents, and the only ceremony was a blessing of Ferdinand on his nephew. Thus Francis Joseph, the personification of monarchical right, ascended his throne in a hole-and-corner manner; this august "crowned head" reigned for nineteen years without any kind of coronation—and was then only crowned King of Hungary. For though the House of Habsburg could rightly claim to be the most historic dynasty in Europe, Hungary was the only part of the Habsburg Empire with a living tradition; yet this tradition was largely of resistance against the Habsburg rulers.

When Francis Joseph took over the throne he exclaimed: "Farewell, my youth!" It was his only human remark. From the first he turned himself into an institution. He sacrificed everything for the sake of the dynasty, and he expected others to sacrifice everything too. Though he had a sincere love for his wife, Elizabeth, the most beautiful woman of her age, he would not extenuate the harsh ritual of Court life even for her. Elizabeth's spirit would not be stifled, and she left him, after providing Catherine Schratt, the Emperor's mistress for more than thirty years and the only human being who came into contact with him and remained human. Elizabeth wandered restlessly across Europe from Corfu to Ireland until she was assassinated by an anarchist on a Lake of Geneva steamer. Rudolph, Francis Joseph's only son, was also driven into wild courses by the repressive Court life and committed suicide at the end of a somewhat sordid romance. Francis Ferdinand, the Emperor's nephew and next heir, married morganatically outside the permitted degrees of royalty. When he and his wife were assassinated at Sarajevo in 1914 the first thought of Francis Joseph was that dynastic purity had been saved: "A higher power has reasserted the rules that I was unable to maintain."

Francis Joseph had no tastes and no friends. Though Vienna was largely built in his reign he set no mark on it; the Imperial buildings are heavy and lifeless. He did nothing to encourage the arts, not even the art of Johann Strauss or of Lehar. Viennese culture, real though frivolous, had no contact with this conscientious worker at his bureaucratic task. His Ministers experienced even more than the usual "thanks of the House of Habsburg." He used them, thrust them forward into conflict, and then, on an impulse or a rumour of failure, would fling them aside. Taaffe, Prime Minister of Austria for fourteen years and the Emperor's boyhood companion, was thus dismissed without explanation or thanks in 1893, and so, in 1906, was Beck, Chief of Staff for thirty years. Francis Joseph ruled without imagination and without winning the hearts of men. After he had been reconciled with the Hungarians and presumably wished to conciliate them he decorated the royal palace at Budapest with scenes of his victories over the Hungarians in 1849. His only thought was of dynastic power. Yet, though rigid in his dynastic aims, he was ready to try any means of sustaining his Empire. He began with military dictatorship and sometimes reverted to it. Taught by defeat, he made concessions to all in turn; the Compromise of 1867 gave Hungary internal independence, and in the same year Austria received a liberal Constitution. Later he sought to win over the Czechs, and finally, in 1907, forced universal suffrage through the Austrian Parliament in order to be able to play off the masses against the middle-class politicians in a vast game of *rouge et noir*. His greatest hatred was for "liberalism" —the attempt to limit the prerogatives of the Crown. Against this liberalism he would call on any ally and would even invoke the rival nationalisms which were tearing his Empire to pieces.

Clever writers in Vienna tried for more than a century to invent an Austrian "mission." This "mission" was supposed to be the security which the Empire gave to fifty million people, in which they could prosper and develop their cultural life. In the twentieth century this "mission" took on a predominantly economic tone, and Austria was praised as a great

"Free Trade area." In truth, the mission was a device by which Hungarian landowners and German capitalists grew rich from the labour of the lesser peoples. It was these two groups whom Francis Joseph took unwillingly into partnership. In his own mind Francis Joseph cared for none of these "missions." He did not regard the dynasty as the servant of the Austrian peoples; it was for them to be the servants of the dynasty and to sustain its military greatness. Viennese intellectuals complained that Francis Joseph did not follow the example of Joseph II, the "people's Emperor." To do this he would have had to lead peasants against their lords and subject peoples, Slav and Rumanian, against the Germans and Magyars, the two privileged nationalities. Such a course was outside dynastic imagining. Francis Joseph was fated to end his reign as a German auxiliary; the only "mission" he left to his successor was to be a German agent—or to disappear.

VII

BISMARCK: THE MAN OF GERMAN DESTINY

OTTO VON BISMARCK was born in 1815 and died on
July 30, 1898. At his birth Prussia was the least of the
Great Powers; when he died Germany already overshadowed
Europe. This was not his doing. Increase of population and
an unrivalled heavy industry made German greatness inevitable; Bismarck's achievement was to keep this greatness
within bounds.

A Conservative by origin and by conviction, he hated
"the deluge" as much as Metternich. Only his method
differed. Metternich resisted the revolution and fell; Bismarck
led the German revolution and mastered it. He used the
phrases of demagogy in order to cheat it of results. He claimed
to have united Germany; in reality he partitioned Germany
with the Habsburgs. He preached the doctrine of military
power; in practice he took only the most limited profit from
the victories over Austria and France, and gave both Powers
another generation of artificial greatness and independence.
He instituted universal suffrage in Germany; he manipulated
it for the benefit of his own class and, most of all, for himself.
While he could not prevent the Germans running mad, he
lured them into a strait-jacket which did not work loose until
twenty years after his fall and was not fully discarded until
forty years after his death.

Bismarck was as deceptive in personality as in policy.
"The Iron Chancellor" was nervous and highly-strung,
given to hysterical weeping and racked with sleeplessness.
Despising writers and artists, he ranks with Luther and
Goethe as a supreme master of German prose and made
every political act a finished performance. He denounced
ideas and won success by manipulating them; he preached
"blood and iron," and pursued European peace; though a
civilian, he always wore military uniform, yet—alone of

German statesmen—asserted the primacy of politicians over the General Staff.

Educated in Berlin by a sophisticated mother, he took on in adult life the rustic airs of his boorish father and paraded a devotion for the family estates which he had rarely seen in youth. From others he demanded absolute sacrifice to duty; he himself as a young man deserted his State post for many months in order to pursue an English girl across Europe and, at the end of his life, betrayed State secrets to the press in order to discredit William II, the master who had dismissed him.

A man of deep emotions, he had no friends, only syco-phants. He despised his supporters even more than he hated his enemies, and ruined the happiness of the son whom he loved because of an old personal feud with the family into which Herbert wished to marry. He had a secure and perfect relationship only with his wife; their love was mutual, yet he joked about the religion which was their closest tie. He made loyalty to the House of Hohenzollern the mainspring of his politics, yet spoke of both William I and William II with boundless contempt and said after his fall: "Were it to do over again, I would be a republican and a democrat." With true genius he expressed the contradictions of the German spirit.

Bismarck made his real entry into politics in 1848 and remained all his life a man of the revolutionary year. Social upheaval and international isolation were his two nightmares. Security was the motive of his policy at home and abroad; and everything he did was an insurance against dangers, some of them imaginary. For many generations the Powers of the circumference—Russia on one side, England and France on the other—had laid down the law to Central Europe. Bismarck isolated Prussia's neighbours, laid down his law in Central Europe, and finally laid down the law for France and Russia as well.

He became Prime Minister of Prussia in 1862. Within two years, he exposed the sham of the Concert of Europe and imposed his will in Schleswig and Holstein, though this involved the deception of the king, of German national feeling of Austria—his ostensible ally—and of the Great Powers. Two years later, in 1866, he lured Russia and France into tolerating the overthrow of the balance of power between Prussia and Austria, on which their own security rested. The battle of Sadova (Königgrätz) made Prussia supreme in Germany; it did not destroy the Habsburg monarchy. Instead Bismarck preserved the Habsburgs, in association with the Magyars, as a barrier against Greater Germany and thus freed Prussia from taking up the German legacy in the Balkans. Similarly in 1870 and 1871, though he isolated France and organized her defeat, he kept victory within bounds; he neither renewed the attempt of Napoleon nor anticipated that of Hitler.

After 1871 Bismarck was the supreme exponent of the balance of power: seeking security for Germany, he gave it to every State in Europe. He would not allow Russia to destroy Austria-Hungary; at the same time he would not support Austrian ambitions in the Balkans. Thanks to Bismarck, the British Empire was never endangered; yet under his patronage France built up an Empire in Africa, and Russia expanded in Central Asia and the Far East. Not only at the Congress of Berlin, but for nineteen years, Bismarck was an honest broker of peace; and his system of alliances compelled every Power, whatever its will, to follow a peaceful course.

Within Germany, too, Bismarck aimed at a balance. With Liberal aid he forced concessions from the Junkers, then reined in the Liberals with Junker support. He first tamed the Roman Catholics by evoking nationalist frenzy, then used the Catholic Centre as a brake on Radical nationalism. Restraining German nationalism was not as easy as restraining foreign Powers. Bismarck's Reich was held together by Junkers who cared nothing for Germany; it treated as enemies the Roman Catholics and the Socialists, who between them represented the German masses. A national State which excluded eight million Germans and a system of universal suffrage which operated against the mass-parties was a political conjuring trick which even Bismarck could not sustain indefinitely. In 1890 he confessed defeat, and William II dismissed him.

Similarly in economic affairs, Bismarck ended in contradiction. He wished to preserve an agricultural Germany of peasants and Junker estates; for the sake of German power, he had to develop German heavy industry, to the ruin of German conservatism, and thus promoted the growth of an urban working-class. Bismarck feared nationalism and socialism; partly by resisting them, partly by compromising with them, he both postponed their victory and made it inevitable.

Bismarck's failure was the failure of conservatism in an age of upheaval. Germany was on the march to world power, and Bismarck could only retard her advance. Nevertheless, no other man could have achieved even his limited and temporary success. The world owes what has been good in the Germany of the last fifty years to Bismarck's policy. In the words of Goethe, *In der Begrenzung zeigt sich der Meister*; his greatness lay in his restraint. The history of modern Europe can be written in terms of three Titans: Napoleon, Bismarck and Lenin. Of these three men of superlative political genius, Bismarck probably did least harm.

VIII

THE RULER IN BERLIN

ON July 31, 1914, Berchtold, Austro-Hungarian Foreign Minister, was dismayed by advice from Bethmann, the German Chancellor, to act with restraint and not to give the signal for war. His distraction was interrupted by Conrad, Chief of the Austrian General Staff. Conrad showed him a telegram from Moltke, Chief of the German General Staff, which urged that Austria-Hungary should at once mobilize against Russia and so launch a European war. Berchtold, with his irresponsible giggle, exclaimed: "That beats everything. Who rules then in Berlin?" This flippant remark was a profound judgment on the Germany of William II, and for that matter on the work of Bismarck. The question baffled contemporaries and has baffled later observers.

Between 1871 and 1890 it had seemed possible to answer the question. Bismarck ruled in Berlin. He devised legislation, determined policy, controlled even the military leaders; his decisions settled Germany's course. Yet Bismarck himself did not give this answer. He always insisted that Germany was ruled by the King of Prussia; and claimed that this was the core of his achievement. Bismarck's answer was not a mere pretence; even he, the greatest of political Germans, shrank from ultimate responsibility and shouldered it on to a "King by the Grace of God." All the same, the version was nonsense in practice, and largely even in theory. Germany could not be ruled by the King-Emperor, as Prussia had been ruled by Frederick the Great or even by Frederick William IV. Men may obey their king, even in a period when monarchical sentiment is declining; they will not obey someone else's king, and the King of Prussia was the king of others for the majority of Germans. The King of Prussia was German Emperor by conquest, by invitation of the German princes, by political intrigue, by constitutional arrangement, by everything except "the Grace of God." The German Emperor had no coronation—hence no religious sanction. Right still counted for much in Germany; and the Emperor's right rested on national sentiment, not on divine appointment.

Bismarck's creation deserved its name of "the second Empire"; its spirit was, in truth, nearer to the demagogy of Napoleon III than to the mystic tradition of "the Holy Roman Empire of the German Nation." After 1806, when the Holy Roman Empire ended, German authority could rest only on the masses. Bismarck had concealed this fact, as the titanic figure of Napoleon I had concealed it in France in similar circumstances. With the fall of Bismarck it could be concealed no longer. The question, "Who rules in Berlin?" was stated with ever-increasing urgency, until it found an answer in 1933.

William II had perhaps supposed in 1890 that he himself would rule in Berlin. This view was held later by those who wished "to hang the Kaiser." The fault of William was his failure to rule, not that he ruled wrongly. Dr. Eyck, his latest historian,[1] is nearer the truth when he draws a parallel with the system of English government in the reign of George III. George III, too, used to be accused of personal rule; this is a myth no longer believed by anyone. On the personal side it is unfair to compare William II with George III. William had considerable political gifts, to say nothing of his gift for phrase-making. Theodore Roosevelt said to him in 1910: "In America you would have your ward behind you and would lead your delegation at your party's national convention." In fact, William was a first-rate "key-note" speaker. On the great issues of politics he often saw farther than his professional advisers. In 1890 he was right to reject Bismarck's programme of a *coup d'état* in favour of reconciling the working-classes to the Reich; in 1905 he was right in opposing Holstein's policy of the Tangier visit; he was right (from the German point of view) in promoting the Baghdad railway; he was right in distrusting the moribund Habsburg monarchy and, at the end, in advocating concessions to Rumania as the one way of staving off disaster; even his advances to both Russia and

---

[1] *Das Persönliche Regiment Wilhelms II*. Politische Geschichte des deutschen Kaiserreiches von 1890 bis 1914. By Erich Eyck.

England did more good than harm—without such a gesture, for example, as his visit to the deathbed of Queen Victoria, estrangement between England and Germany would have come even sooner than it did. While the German Foreign Office was confidently snubbing all the Great Powers in turn, William II saw the dangers of "the free hand" and never ceased, though by erratic impulses, to seek for some great political combination.

His immediate reactions, no doubt, were often as wild as his longer vision was sound. He would scribble, "We must mobilize at once", on the news of some colonial dispute; and even proposed to arrest the transference of the British Fleet to the North Sea by an ultimatum. He exploded repeatedly against Austrian failure to destroy Serbia; yet he realized more clearly than any German diplomatist that this was a futile programme and, in his serious moments, urged reconciliation. His marginal notes, which made so much stir when published, were written for pleasure, not for action; and no action ever followed from them. They were the outbreaks of a man knowing himself, and known to be, irresponsible. The Kruger telegram is a case in point. This was certainly a watering-down of William's original idea of landing marines at Delagoa Bay. All the same, it would never have been sent, had it not suited Holstein's scheme of frightening England with the shadow of a Continental League. When this scheme failed, Marschall and Holstein shifted the blame to William, though the policy underlying it was theirs. So later, in the great crisis of the reign, Germans of all classes, from Bülow downwards, used the *Daily Telegraph* affair as a means for shifting on to William II all the consequences of German arrogance and power.

William II was not a ruler; he was a medium. He reflected the political mind of Germany and expressed it with genius. Contemporary observers were much at fault when they attributed the great German Navy to a personal whim of William II. The Navy was a demagogic cause, promoted by Liberal professors and popular even among Socialist and Roman Catholic voters. Had William surrendered altogether to his demagogic impulses, he would have anticipated Hitler's undisputed power. As it was, his upbringing and conscience reined him in; the King of Prussia restrained the German Emperor, as Prussia, in Bismarck's conception, restrained Germany. These negations were not a solution; and since William failed to lead, the problem was returned to the Chancellors. Here, indeed, is the profound political interest of the reign of William II—the search for a principle of authority and responsibility when this could no longer be provided by the Crown. To return to the analogy with George III: Dr. Eyck supposes that George III was defeated by "the opposition of Charles Fox," and blames the Germans for not producing a Liberal figure of similar eminence. This does that charming gambler too much honour. Growth of a sense of responsibility, not of an opposition, transformed the British Constitution; and this responsibility rested on a governing class which was truly representative of "the political nation." In Bismarckian Germany the governing classes, military and civil, were not merely out of touch with the masses who had now become the nation: they were actively and consciously opposed to everything that was dearest to national ambition. Bismarck's greatest achievement was his defeat of Greater Germany: he preserved the Habsburg monarchy and insisted that his truncated Germany was a "satiated State." This flew in the face of national sentiment. The only binding force in the governing classes was resistance to the popular will. Liberal observers, misled by Western analogies, thought that this implied principally resistance to a constitutional system; but the national masses demanded most of all a truly united Germany.

The reign of William II saw two attempts to break the deadlock between the governing classes and the nation; in different ways both Caprivi and Bülow aspired "to rule in Berlin." Caprivi took the way of Liberalism; Bülow attempted to wield the bow of Bismarck and to create a new Bismarckian compromise by agility and intrigue. Caprivi, who followed Bismarck as Chancellor, has been neglected by historians; yet he was the most significant of Bismarck's successors, for he conducted the experiment in Liberalism which later writers often suggested as the "solution" of the German problem. In fact Caprivi was the only parliamentary Chancellor of Imperial Germany. Though appointed by the Emperor, he thought in terms of a parliamentary majority, and this could be created only by means of a "national" programme. Hence Caprivi gave up Bismarck's negative foreign policy and supported the German cause in south-eastern Europe: domestic and foreign demagogy went hand in hand. Caprivi justified the imperial military programme by reference to Russia, instead of to France; and the climax of his policy came in 1893 when he carried the increased Army grant with the votes of Roman Catholics, Poles and some Progressives. As Dr. Eyck rightly says, the split in the Progressive party which followed this vote marked the end of Liberalism as a political force in Germany. Dr. Eyck calls it suicide; suicide is sometimes the only solution. Liberalism had no future if it failed to support Caprivi; equally it had no future if it supported him. For Caprivi himself had no future. In 1894 he ran into conflict with Botho Eulenburg, Prime Minister of Prussia. Caprivi wanted a democratic reform of the Prussian suffrage, Eulenburg a revival of the anti-Socialist laws. William II took the only course and dismissed them both. The decisive answer was given: no one could rule in Berlin.

This answer was accepted by Hohenlohe, the next Chancellor. Dr. Eyck speaks contemptuously of his age and feebleness; these were the necessary conditions of his existence. As a Bavarian, he would not restrain Germany for the sake of Prussia; as a Conservative, he would not break Prussia for the sake of Germany. With little power over events and no influence in the Reichstag, he tolerated all the decisive lurches in German policy: the Baghdad railway, the great Navy, the establishment in China were all Hohenlohe's doing, or rather consequences of his lack of doing. He deliberately avoided asking the great question, let alone attempting to answer it. Yet it was a question which demanded an answer. The man who attempted to answer it in the reign of William II was Bülow, Chancellor from 1900 to 1909. Bülow's name is weighed down by his *Memoirs*, the most trivial record ever left by a man who has occupied high position. Nevertheless he dominated the history of Wilhelmine Germany. Bülow was the only Imperial Chancellor after Bismarck to count in

German politics—the only one who made effective speeches
and to whom men looked for a "policy." Still more, "the
Bülow *bloc*" of 1906 was the first stable parliamentary combination behind the Chancellor since Bismarck broke with the
National Liberals in 1879, and it was a more reliable coalition
than any created under the Weimar republic. Finally, in 1908,
Bülow—whether deliberately or not—used the *Daily Telegraph*
affair to eject William II from politics and to impose upon
him the limitations of a constitutional monarch. William II
never recovered from this blow; it ended whatever fragments
of "personal rule" remained.

Bülow's success was barren. It served only to reveal that
the problem of German government lay deeper than in
William's character; it was rooted in the foundations of
Bismarck's Reich. The humiliation of William II left Bülow
face to face with the Prussian Conservatives; and once more,
as with Caprivi, it became clear that the twin causes of "world
policy" and internal democracy could be achieved only after
the defeat of the classes which Bismarck had preserved, the
forces of old Prussia. Bülow declared to the Conservatives
who brought him down: "We shall meet again at Philippi."
The engagement was not fought in Bülow's lifetime; it was
won by his demagogic heir in 1933 and completed by the
massacres which followed July 20, 1944. Bülow's fall led to
another, more fateful, interregnum, the Chancellorship of
Bethmann Hollweg. Hohenlohe had allowed policy to be
made without him; Bethmann Hollweg had it made against
him. It was a grotesque, though inevitable, conclusion to
Bismarck's work that the Chancellor should be helpless both
in the Reichstag and in the Prussian Landtag; universal
suffrage and privileged class-franchise alike rejected him.
Yet for this very reason he was the only possible Chancellor.
As in Metternich's Austria, "administration had taken the
place of government."

A solution of a sort was found, perhaps against Bethmann
Hollweg's will: a solution of foreign policy. German foreign
policy of the 1890's had been "cabinet diplomacy," even
though it made an occasional demagogic gesture. The last
display of this "cabinet diplomacy" was the first Moroccan

crisis of 1905, a crisis deliberately engineered by Holstein without any preparation of public opinion and hence ending in failure for Germany. Once more, in the Bosnian crisis, Bülow was the man of the transition: demagogue enough to back the German cause in south-eastern Europe, Bismarckian enough to regret having done so. In 1911 national opinion came into its own: the Agadir crisis was fought with public backing from start to finish. Nevertheless, Agadir was a false start, a red herring: it was deliberately designed by Kiderlen, last of the Bismarckians, to distract German chauvinism from eastern Europe and so from the mortal conflict with Russia. Until Agadir, Germany had remained a Power which, if not "satiated," could still be satisfied with colonial gains; after Agadir, Germany had to bid for the mastery of Europe. This inescapable fate determined the diplomacy of 1913 and 1914, which Dr. Eyck describes in full detail: German policy sought in vain to avoid the mission of conquest which was being thrust upon it. Few historians will quarrel with Dr. Eyck's verdict that the German statesmen and generals did not deliberately plan the outbreak of world war in July 1914; yet a war of conquest was the only possible outcome of German history. Bethmann Hollweg had been the only Imperial Chancellor to be censured by the Reichstag; he was also the only Chancellor to receive from the Reichstag a unanimous vote of confidence. Certainly in August 1914 Bethmann Hollweg did not "rule in Berlin"; what ruled at last in Berlin was the will of the German people for power.

The German problem, past and present, is the problem of German unity. Though this does not exist now, we are tempted to think that it existed in some Golden Age of the past. Dr. Eyck's book is a reminder that this Golden Age cannot be found in the age of William II. Imperial Germany was never a united national State, in the sense that France was united and made a nation by the great revolution. In Imperial Germany, almost as much as in the Holy Roman Empire, there was a balance of authorities and classes; instead of authoritarian rule there was "organized anarchy." Germany had, in some sort, a "governing class"—the Prussian army officers and Prussian administrators. Though this class held

F

Germany together, it was even more concerned to hold
Germany back; while offering Germany a corset, it strapped
on a strait-jacket. The first German war weakened this class;
the Hitler revolution completed its destruction. There are
now no forces within Germany to resist the full programme
of German unification, and the present partition rests solely
on the occupying armies. This gives it a unique and precarious
character. A Germany free from foreign control will seek to
restore the united Greater Germany which Hitler achieved
in 1938; nor will democracy provide an automatic safeguard
against a new German aggression. In the reign of William II
every step towards democracy was a step towards general
war. The Navy was popular, "world policy" was popular,
support for the German cause in eastern Europe was popular.
Attempts at reconciliation with others were unpopular; and
William's prestige was ruined in 1908 when it became known
that he favoured friendship with England.

The harsh truth of German history is that the solution of
the German question cannot be found within Germany.
Partition cannot be maintained as a permanent policy; yet
a united Germany will keep Europe in apprehension, and
would be tolerable only in a world of United Nations.
Wilhelmine Germany overshadowed her neighbours by
playing off East and West; any future Germany will seek
to do the same. If the Great Powers were on friendly terms,
there would even now be no German problem; so long as
they remain estranged, Germany will offer the occasion,
and may be the originator of future wars. "Who rules in
Berlin?" The question once dominated German history; now
it torments all the world. In our impatience and anxiety we
are led to hope that one day the German people may rule in
Berlin. That outcome is, in the long run, unavoidable; it will
be tolerable only if there also rules in Berlin awareness of a
community of nations. It is for the Germans to seek unity on a
democratic and pacific basis; the Great Powers must ensure that
the Germans do not promote unity by a programme of foreign
aggression. At the present time, both the Germans and the
Great Powers are failing in their task; and the question, "Who
rules in Berlin?" has lost nothing of its menacing character.

IX

GERMAN UNITY

WHAT is wrong with Germany is that there is too much of it. There are too many Germans, and Germany is too strong, too well organized, too well equipped with industrial resources. This great Germany is a very recent appearance, created overnight by Bismarck and completed only by Hitler. It is tempting, and perhaps profitable, to look back to the time before this Reich was manufactured, and even to consider whether there are any remnants of a Germany of more normal proportions. The longing for a more manageable Germany accounts for the speculations about German particularism, especially for the theory that German aggression can be explained by the domination of Prussia over the remaining German States. But an historian would hesitate to confirm either this easy theory or these easy solutions.

The mosaic of petty States which conventionally forms the immemorial background of Germany was, in fact, the creation of the Treaty of Westphalia (1648), the outcome of the Thirty Years' War. The Treaty of Westphalia enshrined and made permanent German disunity; but it was not the work of the Germans. Indeed, if Germany had been left to herself the Thirty Years' War would, in all probabilty, have produced a Germany united under the House of Habsburg. Westphalia was the result of foreign interference, the intervention of Denmark, of the Dutch, of Sweden and, above all, of France. The German States were artificially preserved by a balance imposed from without. Few of these States had much historic background; and few of the dynasties had any individual character or long-standing connection with the territories over which they ruled. The object of the system of Westphalia was not the preservation of particular dynasties but the maintenance of dynasticism in general.

In the ensuing century and a half dynasties rose and fell

in importance; some disappeared altogether, one—the Hohenzollern kings of Prussia—came to rank along with the
Habsburg emperors as a European Power. These dynastic
shufflings meant little or nothing to the inhabitants of the
German States. Their attachment was not so much to
particularism as to localism. The inhabitant of Dresden or
of Leïpzig was proud of Dresden or of Leipzig, not of Saxony;
the inhabitant of Heidelberg was proud of Heidelberg, not
of the Palatinate. Particularism helped localism to survive;
only in that sense did it correspond to any German desire.
But German desires were irrelevant; the Westphalia system
was maintained, as it had been imposed, from without.

The Westphalia system was also overthrown from without
by the armies of the French Revolution and the policy of
Napoleon. The French armies defeated first Austria and then
Prussia, and so destroyed the balance on which the old system
had rested. Napoleon wanted more from Germany than the
French monarchy had done. The Bourbons had merely
wanted Germany to be harmless; Napoleon wanted active
German assistance in the furthering of his European plans.
The old system of petty States and Free Cities could not
produce either the men or·the money Napoleon needed.
Quite arbitrarily he eliminated all the smaller units and re-
grouped Germany into some thirty States of medium size;
States impotent to oppose him but respectable enough to be
ranked as allies.

These States, though larger, had no more reality than
before; in fact, thanks to the ruthless redrawing of frontiers
by Napoleon, they had less. The Free Cities and the ecclesiastical States were incorporated territorially in the neighbouring
kingdoms; spiritually they remained unaffected. Napoleon
said the last word on these royal creations of his when he cut
short the attempt of one of them to butt into a conversation
with the Tsar Alexander I: *"Taisez-vous, roi de Bavière."*
The German princes, grouped into the Confederation of the
Rhine, were in law sovereign and independent; in fact they
counted in Napoleon's Empire for as much as did Croatia
or Slovakia in the Empire of Hitler. Their independence
decorated the Empire but degraded themselves.

The defeat of Napoleon brought this short-lived system to an end, and in the general hurly-burly the German States were threatened with total disappearance. But in 1815 a united national Germany was a Jacobinical solution, unacceptable to the victorious Powers. The German States could disappear only if absorbed into an existing Great Power, and in Germany, there were two—Austria and Prussia. Therefore the petty States continued to exist, their existence dependent on the jealousy of Austria and Prussia, not on their own strength. They were grouped now into the German Confederation, a new edition of Napoleon's confederation, with Austria and Prussia substituted for France as the protecting authority.

Life was pleasant in these little States. The inhabitants escaped the burdens of military service and of taxation which they would have had to bear if their preservation had depended on their own efforts; and they enjoyed an affected sham-constitutionalism which they proudly contrasted with Austrian and Prussian autocracy. Thus there came into being the conception of a "third Germany," under the leadership of Bavaria, the most respectable of these States: the Germany of culture and art, free from absolutism and militarism—but free also from reality. The system of 1815, like the system of Westphalia, was imposed from without. Austria and Prussia held each other in check but acted together against any renewed French threat or against any attempt to unite Germany by revolutionary means; and the two great neighbours, Russia and France, were always alert to see that the balance was maintained. The German States owed their existence not to German sentiment but to the determination of the Great Powers.

In 1848 German liberals of the middle class attempted to unite Germany by peaceful constitutional means. They failed: there was no force in the "third Germany" and without force Austria and Prussia could not be eliminated. After 1848 Karl Marx wrote: "Unless the radicals unite Germany by revolutionary means Bismarck will unite it by reactionary Junker means." The reverse was also true: Bismarck set out to conquer Germany for Prussia in order to prevent a radical

Germany which would conquer Prussia. Bismarck talked nationalism; he thought only of the Prussian landed class. This explains the paradox that he allowed the States to continue to exist when he could, apparently, have ended them altogether. If the German States disappeared Prussia too would be swallowed up in a liberal-national Germany; the sham existence of the other States was the guarantee of the continued real existence of Prussia and her Junker lords.

Bismarck had to eliminate one by one the forces which had imposed the settlement of 1815. Russia was bought off, partly by support for Tsarist tyranny in Poland, mainly by acquiescing (or rather appearing to acquiesce) in her Balkan plans. England did not need to be bought off: absorbed in the pursuit of wealth, she had renounced interest in continental affairs. Austria was isolated and, in 1866, defeated in war. The German Confederation ceased to exist; most of the north German States were annexed to Prussia and the other States north of the Main were incorporated into a new federation, which amounted to annexation to Prussia in all but name. The military efforts of the southern States in 1866 had shown that by their own strength they could not exist for a day. But Napoleon III insisted that they should remain independent, and on French orders they enjoyed four years as "internationally independent States."

In 1870 Bismarck dealt with France as he had dealt with Austria: isolated diplomatically, she was then defeated in war. For the first time since the early seventeenth century a single authority ruled in Germany, secure from foreign interference, and could dispose of Germany as it wished. But Bismarck wished for a conservative Germany, a Germany of princes and nobles, not an egalitarian Germany of nationalist liberals. All Germany could, no doubt, have been incorporated in Prussia; but then Prussia would have been incorporated in Germany. Prussian needs kept the German States in existence.

The States which joined the Empire in 1871 received greater concessions than had been given in 1867. Bavaria in particular kept not only her own postal system but controlled her own railways and had, in peace-time, a separate army

command. The Federal Council, nominated by the State
Governments, was, in theory, the governing body of the
Empire, in which policy was decided; the Reich had limited
defined powers; apart from the yield from Customs dues it
had no independent income, but was dependent on deficiency
grants from the member States. In form, indeed, the Reich
was no more than a federation of princes, with the King of
Prussia as President. But it was a federation in which the
President could always call the tune: he commanded the
armed forces, he nominated the Chancellor, for all practical
purposes he could interpret the Constitution as it suited his
needs, the deficiency grants had to be provided. The States
survived just as long as their existence suited the aims of the
Prussian governing class.

The first German war exposed the artificiality of this
federal structure. The States were told nothing of the causes
of the war, nor of its aims; and Germany fought the war
under the dictatorship of the High Command without ever
noticing that the States still existed. In 1918 defeat destroyed
the basis of Bismarck's elaborate compromise and seemed to
give a new chance to the liberal forces which had failed in
1848. The Left majority of Socialists and Liberals in the
Constituent Assembly at Weimar desired a unitary Germany;
they knew that the States expressed the class structure of old
Germany, not the sentiments of the peoples.

But this Left majority, though sincere in its beliefs, was
even more anxious to conciliate the Right parties and so to
present a solid "national" front against the victorious Allies.
The Right feared a Socialist Germany and therefore defended
the States, Bavaria above all, as a means of limiting the
democracy of the Central Government. The States were
advocated as a deliberately reactionary measure; and hostility
to "Versailles" made the Left abandon their liberal convictions. Once more the States owed their existence to external
forces. An attempt was made to regroup the States on regional
lines; but the project came to nothing, and the States remained,
more senseless than ever; explicable only on dynastic grounds,
they had lost their dynasties and yet continued to exist.

The German States under the Weimar Republic had no

real power. Only Bavaria aspired to play an independent role, half-farcical, half-gallant, as the rallying-point of the conservative and "national" forces against the "Marxist" Reich. The high-water mark of this performance was Hitler's attempt at a national revolution in Bavaria in 1923. But Hitler's coup came too late (and too early). Germany had now a strong Government under Stresemann; and his first action was to explode the myth of Bavarian separatism. After 1923 the Weimar Republic was a unitary system, the States enjoying a twilight existence only because of the respect felt by the Parliamentary politicians for the letter of the Constitution.

Once this respect vanished the States vanished too. In 1932 the Socialist Government of Prussia was brusquely ordered out of existence by Von Papen; it protested—and obeyed. In 1933 Bavaria tried to revive its independent performance, this time as the rallying-point for the forces of legality; the performance did not last twenty-four hours. In May 1933, Hitler brought the German States to an end: they remained as administrative units, and that only for some purposes, but in a Germany without rights the States were without rights too.

Thus the German States have always been as much artificial, as much manufactured, as the Reich; they have always been imposed upon Germany from without. It is sometimes proposed to revive them in order to save the victorious Allies the burden of policing Germany, but the moment the Allies cease to police Germany the revived States will collapse. It is more practicable to make Germany's neighbours strong than to make Germany weak.

X

FRENCH NORTH AFRICA: CREATION OF A CENTURY

Frenᴄʜ Nᴏʀᴛʜ Aғʀɪᴄᴀ has been conquered and organized within a century, yet this great achievement is as much evidence of the decline of France's European position as of the development of her Imperial power. After 1815 France could never hope again to rival, let alone surpass, the empire of Napoleon; never again would her frontier touch the Vistula or the Gulf of Cattaro. Yet she still desired to be great; she sought glory without exertion, victory without risk, an ersatz Empire, and she found it in the project, attempted by Bonaparte though soon abandoned, of renewing the unifying work of Rome in the Mediterranean.

Bonaparte's Egyptian expedition of 1798 foreshadowed French North Africa, both in its policy of combining traditional rule with revolutionary ideas—the caïd draped in a tricolour sash—and in its motive of creating an empire without encountering either European resistance or the British Fleet. In this it failed, brought instead Russia into the Second Coalition and Nelson to Aboukir Bay. Yet though Egypt was lost the idea of French North Africa was born.

In 1829 Charles X, last Bourbon king of France, was driving into a political conflict with the French people; determined to restore the old system of privilege and absolute monarchy, he sought to distract popular attention by the pursuit of glory and dispatched an expedition to conquer Algiers. The conquest succeeded, though the plan failed: Algiers, a pirate stronghold, was no substitute for the Rights of Man, and in July 1830 Charles X lost his throne. But Algiers remained French. England, alone of the Great Powers, was concerned for the Mediterranean, but though she might well have resisted Charles X she was far too anxious to

Thru Palmerston

promote the stability of Louis Philippe, the new constitutional king, to raise difficulties about the occupation of Algiers.

That initial foothold once secured, expansion necessarily followed: Arab tribes, bandits and brigands, could only be restrained by a ceaseless advance of the frontier of civilization; yet the process was so imperceptible that at no point could England call "Halt!" and declare that the balance of power in the Mediterranean was being disturbed. The Algerian campaigns continued throughout the July Monarchy and the Second Empire, providing generals with a reputation which subsequent experiences in Europe did not always justify. Bugeaud and Lamoricière, MacMahon and Bazaine swaggered through the streets of Paris as though returning from Austerlitz or the Beresina; those who survived until 1870 were to show the cheapness of Algerian glory.

The catastrophe of 1871 so dazed France as to leave her temporarily even without colonial ambitions. The great majority of Frenchmen no longer desired even a substitute glory; they desired only quiet, to be left alone in Europe, to be ignored. The new advocates of Imperial expansion were not, as is often supposed, friends of Germany, seeking to distract France from the line of the Vosges; the greatest of them, Gambetta and Ferry, had honourable careers as enemies of Germany. They preached a vigorous colonial policy in the hope that overseas France would recover her confidence and would make there the faltering steps of a convalescent, preparatory to raising the questions that "were reserved for the future."

The opposition to colonial expansion, always strong in France, sprang from no principle of anti-Imperialism, still less from a desire to engage in conflict with Germany in Europe; it was merely resentment at being reminded that France had been or could ever be a Great Power. Thus the French had to be cajoled into accepting colonial gains with the assurance that there was no danger, and at the first sign of risk drew back. Only the need for France in the balance of power brought her great gains at little cost.

Tunis, its port of Bizerta dominating the Central Mediterranean, was a reward for French reserve at the Congress of Berlin. Bismarck, anxious to keep France contented and aloof from Russia, proposed she should take Tunis; England, herself acquiring Cyprus, agreed to the compensation; and Russia, needing France in the future, could do no less. Only Italy, forgotten by all, protested when France occupied Tunis in 1881, and has done so ever since. But Tunis, though valuable, was a trifle; ever since 1798 Egypt had been the ultimate aim of French Mediterranean policy, and France had created there a cultural and economic lead, culminating in the building of the Suez Canal by French capital in the 'sixties.

In Egypt, France now met her greatest setback; she failed to snatch it resolutely for herself, jibbed in 1882 at co-operating there with England, and so lost all chance of making real the legacy of Bonaparte. Thereafter for twenty years the French sought to dislodge England from Egypt by soft words, by intrigue, by diplomatic combinations, by threat, but when in 1898 it became clear that England could be dislodged only by war the French drew back, for if indeed they were fated to fight a large-scale war once more it would not be for Egypt and the mastery of the Mediterranean but for Alsace-Lorraine and the liberty of Europe that they would abandon their repose. Unable to oust England, in 1904 the French wisely came to terms and so created the Entente.

At the other end of the Mediterranean the French were more successful. Here, too, a Mohammedan State, once strategic master but now derelict, drifted towards collapse, and France, neighbour of Morocco since 1847, carried on steady frontier encroachments which she hoped would be imperceptible. But here, too, she encountered England, who saw in Moroccan independence the best security for Gibraltar. The French tactic was to deprive England of the support of others: to buy off Italy in 1900 with the promise of worthless Libyan desert, to hold out dazzling prospects to Spain, to ensure (as she thought) the indifference of Germany. Then France waited for the collapse of the Moorish authority, which came in 1902. England cut her losses: insisted that the Mediterranean coastline of Morocco should go to Spain and let the rest go in return for French agreement in Egypt.

But the French exulted too soon. Germany, with no serious Moroccan interests, but determined to destroy the Entente, abandoned Bismarck's policy of encouraging France everywhere except on the Vosges and came to the defence of a fictitious Moroccan independence. Twice Germany threatened a European crisis; twice France temporized and paid a price for manufactured German claims; twice France was sustained only by the assurance of British support. In 1911 French claims to Morocco received at last general recognition, but the French drew the conclusion that if they were to encounter German opposition everywhere, then better encounter it at the most vital spot. The *réveil national* of 1912 was the assertion that France could be great overseas only if she were great in Europe.

In the years after 1933 this lesson was again lost. France attempted to withdraw into her empire, this time to abdicate without waiting for defeat, though in fact defeat was not spared her. The French empire in Africa, despite its achievements, can never be more than a consolation for European glories, and Frenchmen count it the sole glory of France only when they despair of her European future. The destiny of France is determined on the Rhine, not in the Atlas Mountains. As a French general said to a colonial enthusiast of the 'eighties: "If you were to bring me all the empires of Asia and Africa they would not in my eyes be worth an acre of the land where I fought in 1870 and where the cuirassiers of Reichshoffen and the Zouaves of Froeschwiller lie."

XI

FASHODA

ON September 19, 1898, Kitchener—fresh from his destruction of Dervish power at Omdurman a fortnight before—encountered a small French force at Fashoda, on the Upper Nile. Kitchener had behind him a victorious army; Marchand, the French commander, a handful of men. France was at the worst moment of the Dreyfus case; her Army was distrusted and confused; her Navy had declined after a period of reform in the previous decade. Russia, her ally, was absorbed in China and indifferent to the affairs of the Near East. In England, Imperialism was at its height. The British Government rested on a compact majority: Chamberlain, as always, was for resolute action, and Salisbury had long planned to restore in Egypt his waning fame. British naval preponderance was greater than ever in our history: the Navy was able to hold the seas against France without special precautions, and the total extra cost of the Fashoda crisis over peace-time estimates was £13,600. For this sum England gained undisputed mastery in the Near East from her only traditional rival. No empire has ever been won so cheaply. Yet the abiding importance of the Fashoda affair was in the affairs of Europe; and the fate of Marchand ultimately turned the scales in the balance of power.

In regard to Egypt and the Sudan, Fashoda was an epilogue, the inevitable conclusion of an old theme. The issue was not whether France or England should control Egypt (and so the Near East). That issue had been decided against France in 1798 when Nelson destroyed Bonaparte's ships at the Battle of the Nile; it had been decided in favour of England in 1882 when the British occupied Egypt without French co-operation. The sole issue was whether France was to receive compensation for renouncing the legacy which Bonaparte had failed to bequeath to her. Unable to challenge the British directly in Egypt, the French had planned to disturb them from the rear by arriving unexpectedly in the Sudan. The basis of this plan was the assumption that it would be easy to dam the Upper Nile and so to dominate Egypt.

This assumption was wrong; and the discovery that even if Marchand stayed in Fashoda he could not carry out this threat was the last blow to French plans. The French assumed, too, that the dispute would always be conducted on a diplomatic and legal plane—a game of chess, as it were, with strict rules. The legal issue was simple (except that the disputants changed sides during the dispute). Since the Egyptian withdrawal from the Sudan in 1885 the British had treated former Egyptian territory as without an owner, *res nullius*. They took part of it for themselves and claimed more; they gave some to the Italians and proposed to lease a large section to Leopold II, king of the Belgians. Against this the French maintained the rights of the Khedive and even of the Sultan, his overlord. Once the French arrived on the Nile they abandoned this argument and, in their turn, insisted that Fashoda was ownerless. The British had reconquered the Sudan in the name of Egypt and in their own as well. At Fashoda they were doubtful of their own rights, since in 1894 they had attempted to lease it to Leopold II (as a barrier against France). For this reason Kitchener hoisted only the Egyptian flag at Fashoda, and not the Union Jack as well, as at Khartum. Still, the legal issue was irrelevant; the British had abandoned it in favour of a decision by force. As Salisbury said: "We claim the Sudan by right of conquest, because that is the simplest and most effective." The French could not compete with this right; Marchand withdrew in November 1898, and the French renounced all access to the Nile Valley in March 1899. The British had far more trouble with Leopold II, who would not renounce his lease (anti-French and so now purposeless) until 1906.

Fashoda completed British security in Egypt and so revolutionized British Near Eastern policy. Once established at Alexandria, the British no longer feared Russian control of Constantinople. The greatest obstacle to better relations between England and Russia was removed; and therewith England severed the last link of interest which held her to the Central Powers. It was the end of the system of associations which had sprung from the Congress of Berlin in 1878.

Fashoda and its outcome also modified French policy towards Russia. Until 1898 it had been possible to dream of a grandiose Franco-Russian action which would give Constantinople to Russia and Egypt to France. This dream was without substance. The French, patrons and creditors of Turkey, would pay too high a price for Egypt if they handed over control of Turkey to Russia; and, in any case, the Russians were not interested—Chinese ambitions eclipsed the Near East. Thus Fashoda emptied the Franco-Russian alliance of the anti-British purpose which it had originally possessed; thereafter it could only be anti-German.

Here, in Franco-German relations, was the true significance of the Fashoda crisis. France had always been torn between continental and overseas interests; and so had missed success in both. Conflict with England had deprived Napoleon of empire in Europe; danger from across the Rhine had kept the French out of Egypt in 1798, in 1840 and in 1882. Had there been no war of 1870 and no question of Alsace and Lorraine, France would certainly have bid again for Egypt; the Suez Canal was purely a French enterprise, and Napoleon III had presided at its opening in 1869. In 1884 Bismarck had reproached the French that they would not play *le grand jeu* in Egypt; they would not engage in a struggle for existence against England in the Near East. The supreme German blunder was to suppose that there was for France any "great game" other than the maintenance of French independence and the redress of the national wrong. The French expeditions to the Upper Nile were designed to wind up the Egyptian affair on honourable terms, not to open "the great game"; and Delcassé, maker of the Anglo-French entente in 1904, was consistent when as Minister of the Colonies he launched the French explorers in 1894. Admittedly Delcassé put out feelers for German support at the height of the Fashoda crisis; the condition for accepting this support was autonomy for Alsace and Lorraine.

Even without this, German diplomatic backing for France would have had immeasurable effect on French public opinion; it was the last, and greatest, opportunity at which the Germans might have established a peaceful hegemony of Europe. Instead, the Germans encouraged both sides to war and believed that the European situation was turning ever more in their favour. In reality, Fashoda and its outcome made the Anglo-French entente inevitable; hence Delcassé insisted from the beginning that France had received fair treatment. Ultimately, in 1904, France got better terms than she could have expected in 1898; this was partly the result of the Boer War, partly of local circumstances in Morocco. The basic terms had been settled in 1898 and remained unaltered. France renounced the Near East in order to maintain her independence in Europe; equally, though less obviously, England, by accepting the French renunciation, became the guarantor of French independence. More than any other single event, Fashoda fixed the pattern of the Triple Entente and so of the war of 1914.

XII

THE ENTENTE CORDIALE

THE agreements which gave formal expression to the Anglo-French entente were published on April 8, 1904. British opinion welcomed the agreements enthusiastically, but saw in them colonial arrangements and nothing more. "We have settled our differences with France" was the common phrase. England had made a good bargain: apart from the sorting out of many minor disputes she had made her control of the two ends of the Mediterranean secure from French interference for ever. At the one end France recognized British predominance in Egypt and finally renounced her own claims; at the other end France gave new guarantees for the invulnerability of Gibraltar, for she agreed, as the condition of her bringing Morocco into the French Empire, that the Moorish coastline opposite Gibraltar should pass to Spain and should be preserved unfortified by the three Powers.

No wonder the British welcomed the agreements: in cheering the French they were, in characteristic British fashion, cheering a good loser. The heirs of Napoleon were acknowledging finally the victory of Nelson. There was on the British side hardly a shade of precaution against Germany. The British were, of course, glad to escape from the attitude of dependence on Germany into which the danger of conflict with France had sometimes led them. But they did not fear Germany, nor had they any cause of conflict with her: the trivial colonial disputes were long ended, and although the building of the German fleet was a nuisance the British were confident that they could always hold their own at sea unaided —after all, in 1905 the British Navy attained a superiority over the combined naval forces of all other Powers unparalleled in our history.

Still less was there on the British side any great principle, any idea of co-operation between the Western democracies against German militarism. Lord Lansdowne, the Foreign Secretary, had worked as hard in 1901 for an alliance with Germany as in 1903 and 1904 for an entente with France. It would be difficult to see in the Irish landowner who resigned from Gladstone's Government in 1880 rather than acquiesce in Irish land reform and the Tory die-hard who defended the House of Lords in 1910 a champion of democracy; and the author of the Lansdowne peace letter, who in 1916 advocated a *status quo* peace (for the sake of social order) and even then saw no need for Germany to atone for her crimes, detected no threat to civilization in the Germany of 1904.

With the French it was far otherwise: there the advocates of the entente knew what they were doing, knew that they were staking the future of France for the sake of Western democratic civilization. For more than two hundred years the French had carried on colonial conflicts with England, and for more than two hundred years French ambitions in Europe had made her the loser in these colonial conflicts. French domination in Europe was ended at Leipzig and Waterloo, and its last echoes were silenced at Sedan. After 1871 necessity left France free as never before to pursue colonial aims and to find a substitute for lost European glory in the Mediterranean empire which was the legacy of Bonaparte's expedition to Egypt in 1798. Germany, as Bismarck was constantly urging, was eager for reconciliation, and if France had been reconciled with Germany as Austria-Hungary had been after 1866 she could have had German support against England in Egypt as Austria-Hungary had it against Russia in the Near East.

Reconciliation was the logical, easy course, but it was not taken. Only a small unpopular minority advocated revenge. The great majority recognized that France had been irretrievably defeated, yet they would not accept German patronage. For almost thirty years France refused to acknowledge the inevitable; she tried to oust the British from Egypt without German support. The Fashoda crisis of 1898 showed that the attempt was impossible, and Delcassé, then newly Foreign Minister, determined the future destinies of France when, without appealing for German assistance, he ordered Marchand to withdraw.

For the English the entente had no anti-German point, but the French knew that in making the entente they were becoming the hostage of democracy on the continent of Europe. They had no hope of winning British assistance for a war of revenge. Indeed, in the then state of the British Army they did not even value British assistance for a defensive war; the Army of their Russian ally remained their sole military support. But the French were determined not to become partners in the German order. To renounce Egypt was a crime against the memory of Bonaparte; to renounce Alsace and Lorraine would be a crime against the national principle, an infringement of the Rights of Man.

The French hesitated for thirty years, but at the crisis of their destiny they remained faithful to the ideas of the Revolution. Relinquishing material gain and Mediterranean empire, they chose to remain independent and to remain democratic; they continued to be the standard-bearers of Western civilization against militarism and autocracy. They chose with their eyes open; they knew that if they held out against German temptation it was on them that the German blow would fall. By making the Anglo-French entente the French brought on themselves the sufferings of 1914–18 and of 1940–44, but in 1904 the prospect of a German hegemony of Europe achieved by peaceful means vanished for ever.

Small wonder that the French hesitated. Small wonder that the entente was not received on the French side with the easy popularity which it evoked in England. Small wonder that at first the nerve of the French almost failed and that, fifteen months after the conclusion of the entente, Delcassé, its author, was driven from office on German orders. Yet the work of Delcassé was not undone. France looked the dangers in the face and, when the time came, accepted them. Many Frenchmen contributed to this decision. Yet Delcassé was more than their spokesman. He was not a great man; indeed, in some ways he was foolish and hot-headed. He offended his own colleagues and injured his own cause. But he had in him the flame of loyalty to the ideas of 1789, to the principles of national independence and of human equality. He was determined to keep France free, both at home and abroad. The entente was perhaps no more than a new expression of the unity of Western democratic civilization, but Delcassé gave it that expression. Forty years after, all those Englishmen who recognize the difference between French civilization and German order may well say: "Homage to Theophile Delcassé!"

XIII

THE SECRET OF THE THIRD REPUBLIC

THE Third Republic puzzled contemporary observers; now it baffles the historian. The Revolution, the Empire or the Monarchy of July can be reduced to a formula; the Third Republic defies definition. It is much easier to describe the forces which threatened it than to discover those which preserved it; hence French historians have written brilliantly on Boulangism, on Royalism or on the revolutionary Syndicalists. It is even possible to explain the origins of the Third Republic; but its founders, whether Thiers or Gambetta, would have been astonished at its development. Inaugurated with radical phrases, it gave France the most conservative system of government in Europe; established by the massacre of Parisian workers, it was the first Great Power to have Socialist ministers, and at the beginning of the twentieth century the leader of the Socialist party was its greatest parliamentarian; repudiating the Empire that had preceded it, it made France the second Imperial Power in the world; born of defeat, it recovered for France the Rhine frontier which two Emperors had lost. Despite its feeble origins, it gave France within fifty years the highest position she had held in Europe since the days of Louis XIV. Twenty years after this achievement, it brought France lower than she had ever been in modern times. The Third Republic went from the greatest success to the worst defeat; yet it had no other aim than compromise and a quiet life.

The most baffling period in this baffling story is that of the national revival between 1912 and 1914. Within these two years France abandoned the policy of conciliation towards Germany and claimed again the position of a Great Power; thus she acquired the vitality which enabled her to withstand not only the first shock of the German attack, but still more the shock of Verdun and of the failure of Nivelle; to survive, despite many alarms, until at last the elderly Clémenceau seemed to give her at last a new youth. Clémenceau became war-dictator; all the same Clémenceau was not a characteristic figure of the Third Republic, and the study of his career throws no light upon it. Rather he was the enemy of all that the Third Republic represented and passed his life attacking its ministers. When he was criticized for this, he replied: "Bah! I have always overthrown the same ministry." The antagonism was clear to him, though not always to his opponents.

It is Caillaux, not Clémenceau, the "traitor," not the dictator, who should be studied; it is Agadir, not the victories of 1918, which express the spirit of the Third Republic. Its secret, if it is to be found anywhere, will be found in Caillaux's *Memoires*,[1] the two first volumes of which were published during the occupation and the third in July 1947. This is not an impartial contribution. It is a subtly delayed revenge against the men who brought Caillaux to ruin, above all, against Poincaré and Clémenceau who, according to Caillaux, by asking too much of France ruined the Third Republic. Caillaux promises revelations; all he gives is the warmed-up gossip of the Palais Bourbon. The reader, half-recollecting Caillaux's story, opens the book full of sympathy for its author; by the end he has almost been convinced that the charges made against Caillaux must have some foundation.

Caillaux, however, does not present himself as a topic of controversy; rather, caught in the storm, he has tried to brave it. The first volume is the story of the days of easy success, when nothing seemed to threaten the stability of the Third Republic. Caillaux was not a Republican by family origin or by education, and still less a Radical Socialist. His father had been a minister in Broglie's government of "May 16" (1877); Caillaux himself began in the Inspectorate of Finance. He was essentially a man of order, hating excess and violence, whether Bonapartist or Republican; he became a Radical, when he saw that the lower middle class and the peasants

[1] *Mes Memoires*. I. Ma Jeunesse orgueilleuse, 1863–1909. II. Mes audaces. Agadir 1909–12. III. Clairvoyance et force d'âme dans les Épreuves, 1912–30. By Joseph Caillaux.

had become the governing classes. His father approved this step: "One must go with the governing forces of one's country." The same argument would have made Caillaux a loyal servant of the Bourbons or of the Directory. Caillaux entered politics as a "government man"; he had the good luck to become, almost at once, Minister of Finance under Waldeck-Rousseau. Caillaux perhaps exaggerates the work and character of this parliamentarian whom he presents as a great man. He hints at an apostolic succession of Radical leaders: Waldeck-Rousseau, Rouvier, Caillaux, patriots though pacific, whose work was destroyed by ambitious "warmongers." Certainly if Caillaux is to be judged by his own account of the years between 1898 and 1909, he must be recognized as the best Minister of Finance in the Third Republic. There is one surprising point: from 1906 to 1909 Caillaux was a minister in the government of Clémenceau. He supposed that Clémenceau had been tamed by the bitter years which followed the Panama scandal; he thought that Clémenceau had become, like the others, a good Republican. Despite this, Caillaux strikes a false note. He cannot refrain from anticipating later events and from producing in advance the stories that he had accumulated over the years. He claims that in 1928 Briand told him that the faults of the Treaty of Versailles were due to the fact that "Clémenceau was not free in relation to England." It is difficult to decide whether this story reflects more discredit on Briand or on Caillaux; and it is typical of the "proofs" which Caillaux claims to furnish.

One episode disturbed the quiet of the first decade of the century: the Moroccan crisis of 1905. Caillaux passes rapidly over this topic, attributing the dispute entirely to Delcassé's failure to inform Germany of his Moroccan plans. This is essential to his later argument. If he once admitted that the German object in 1905 was to reduce France to a position of dependence, the policy of Agadir would be condemned in advance. Agadir is the subject of Volume II, the least interesting of the three volumes. The revelations, for what they are worth, have already appeared in Caillaux's earlier book on this subject; they are merely repeated here with more bitterness. Caillaux was at least consistent: having once taken up a line of defence, he neither changed nor added to it, even in a book to be published after his death. Thus there is nothing new concerning the unofficial approach which he made to Germany; nothing on the projects of economic collaboration between Germany and France to which he aspired; and very little on his schemes for acquiring Spanish Morocco with German assistance. His attitude towards England is the strangest feature in his account of Agadir. The English statesmen aimed to show their firm determination to support France; Caillaux represents himself as abandoned by England and extracting from the English statesmen only a reluctant acquiescence. The Agadir crisis was certainly a turning-point in British foreign policy: the moment at which British opinion in general became convinced that it was Germany's ambition to dominate Europe. Caillaux cannot admit this ambition; therefore in his defence he talks only of Morocco, which he justly claims to have won for France without a war. This was not as great an achievement as he makes out. France could have had Morocco whenever she liked on Germany's terms; and Caillaux seemed to have accepted those terms.

This should have been his real defence, except that it was impossible to use it after all that followed. It was the logical development of the beginnings of the Third Republic that France did not challenge the position of Germany in Europe, but contented herself with empire in Africa; this was the policy of Gambetta and of Ferry, the one policy that could combine glory and peace. Caillaux is in the right when he presents his Agadir policy as that of a good Republican in the old sense; even his secret negotiations had their precedents in Gambetta's advances to Bismarck. But times had changed. Instead of being hailed as a great Republican statesman, Caillaux was driven from power, never again to be Prime Minister. French history reached its most dramatic and unexpected turning-point since the Revolution. Caillaux explains his defeat by intrigue and corruption. These played their part, but far more decisive was the unconscious refusal of French sentiment to accept a subordinate place in Europe.

This was shown by the sequel. Caillaux never realized that his chance had passed. In 1914, he was still dreaming of a pacific coalition between Radicals and Socialists, the coalition of Jaurès and Caillaux; this, he claims, would have refused to support Russia in the Balkans and so prepared the way for a Franco-German co-operation to impose peace on Russia and Austria-Hungary. Jaurès was blinded by his preoccupation with electoral reform. Nevertheless, Caillaux insists, the coalition would have been made, had it not been for the calumnies of Calmette and his assassination by Mme. Caillaux. It is typical of Caillaux's vanity that he should find in his private affairs the cause of the first German war, typical also of that lack of a sense of reality which finally brought the Third Republic to disaster. The story of Calmette is told in detail, the most surprising element being the affirmation that the press campaign was inspired by Poincaré, Barthou and Klotz (the last name being added to make the first two seem less improbable). Certainly Poincaré and Barthou were glad to see Caillaux excluded from public life. In May 1913 Poincaré said to Paléologue: "Clémenceau detests me. . . . Yet despite his great faults of pride and jealousy, of resent-ment and hate, he has one quality which earns him forgiveness, a quality which Caillaux lacks: he has, in the highest degree, national fibre, he is a patriot like the Jacobins of 1793." Caillaux never understood that between 1912 and 1914 France transcended the Third Republic and rejected for ever his policy of conciliation towards Germany.

Curiously enough his energy and self-confidence flag when he comes to talk of the period of the war. Yet it was in 1916 and not in 1914 that Caillaux offered a terrible alternative to the policy of making war. In 1914 all France was deter-mined to resist German domination; by the end of 1916 her effort seemed exhausted. A party of peace came into existence with Caillaux at its head. If Poincaré had appointed Caillaux instead of Clémenceau, a compromise peace would have been attempted. It is inconceivable that Caillaux did nothing, that he attempted no peace propaganda, that he made no contact, however indirect, with the Germans. There is not a word of it in his *Memoirs*. Even stranger, Clémenceau, though still hated, becomes in Volume III a great figure beyond the reach of insults and, almost, the saviour of his country. It is as though Caillaux acknowledged the greatness of his adversary and admitted defeat. Henceforth he reserves his spite for Poincaré, certainly a figure of less importance, but who also had his moment of greatness when he determined to place Clémenceau in power. The story of the peace that failed, the negotiations of 1917, has still to be written; when it is written Caillaux will fill a larger place in it than he claims for himself in his *Memoirs*. This was the last chance of the old Europe and of the historic Great Powers, of Austria-Hungary and France. To succeed, Caillaux would have had to be very different from what he was: less intelligent and less subtle, but also more honest and more patriotic.

Where Caillaux failed after Agadir, Briand succeeded at Locarno and Bonnet at Munich—both attempts to save the continent of Europe by a reconciliation between France and Germany. Caillaux could have claimed to be the John the Baptist of these two strokes and even of the policy of Montoire, which was their last version. Yet though a "government man," Caillaux had in him a strange streak of obstinacy and contradiction. A financier from the upper middle class, he had turned against his origin and, becoming a Radical, had represented a peasant constituency; he had preached reconciliation with Germany at the moment of national revival; he had intrigued for peace during the first German war. Towards the end of his life, he refused to believe in the policy of collaboration with the Germany of Hitler, although this was the official policy of the governing class. Certainly he had no faith in French resistance or in the return of past glory. Like many others, he accepted the government of Vichy and hoped that France, once liberated by her great allies, would then be reconciled with a more civilized Germany. Thus he remained to the end faithful to the policy of Agadir; and to the end he saw in his opponents only warmongers bent on the ruin of Europe.

Only a Franco-German reconciliation could have given Europe peace and stability; this was the core of truth in the policy of Agadir. The mistake was to suppose this reconciliation possible. The Third Republic was Radical though pacific, and its leaders, whether Ferry, Caillaux or Bonnet, believed that in Germany too the policy of war was supported only by a few militarists and by the Kaiser. In reality expansion, if not war, was essential to the German system, and every step towards the rule of the masses increased German violence. A peaceful collaboration was possible only with the German Conservatives, as between Ferry and Bismarck or Caillaux and Kiderlen. This class was losing ground, and there was no Conservative with whom Bonnet could collaborate: he had to pretend to find an aristocrat in Ribbentrop and Bismarckian moderation in Goering. The Third Republic had to choose between Radicalism and Pacifism. In 1914 and 1917, in the strange atmosphere of the national revival, it gave up Pacifism, and Caillaux represented the defeated party. In 1940 it gave up Radicalism and, in fact, ceased to exist for the sake of reconciliation with Germany. This sacrifice only served to show that the policy of Agadir could not have saved the Third Republic and its contradictions. If France had followed Caillaux in 1911, in 1914, or in 1917, she would have been cut off from England and Russia and would have given Germany the mastery of Europe without a struggle. It needed two German wars to repudiate the policy of Agadir, wars which brought the ruin of France, but which ruined Germany as well. The stability of the Continent was and remains possible only at the price of German hegemony. This price France refused to pay, whatever the consequences to herself. The French decision saved Europe from German domination. It was the last great service which France performed for European civilization before herself ceasing to be a Great Power.

XIV

TANGIER IN DIPLOMACY

I n international relations, acts and professions do not always coincide; when there is a downright conflict the result is a problem apparently "insoluble." For the last forty years Tangier has been such a problem, one makeshift solution after another rigged up and then discarded. Tangier is undeveloped and unfortified; if it were fortified and given both harbour and airfields it would eclipse Gibraltar. Potentially it is the key to the Mediterranean; that is the Tangier problem. The fine phrases of 1904 asserted that the Entente was a reconciliation with France, a settlement of all differences; in reality the Anglo-French agreement rested on the determination of each that the other should not have Tangier. Before 1904 England, on easy terms with Germany and indifferent to French friendship, had been the encroaching Power; even as late as 1901 the Foreign Office assumed that when Morocco fell to pieces England would acquire Tangier with German assistance. Once England abandoned the idea of a German alliance she became at Tangier the negative Power; her aim was to keep France out of Tangier and yet be on friendly terms with France. The French aim has been broadly the opposite—to remain on friendly terms with England and yet to get into Tangier. So far the British policy has succeeded, but only by shifts increasingly precarious and discreditable.

The solution of 1904 was that Spain should be interposed between French Africa and Gibraltar. The Anglo-French agreement of April 8, 1904, laid down that all the coastline of Morocco from the frontier of Algeria to a point far down the Atlantic (including, that is, Tangier) should go to Spain. An agreement between France and Spain followed in October 1904, and into this the French inserted a new provision: "The town of Tangier shall keep the special character which is given to it by the presence of the Diplomatic Corps and by its municipal and sanitary institutions." This clause was approved without much reflection by the British Government; it probably did not occur to it that when Morocco became predominantly a French protectorate the Diplomatic Corps would lose its importance. In 1911 Morocco fell to pieces; Germany was bought off by France after the crisis of Agadir; and in 1912 the French and Spanish protectorates were brought into being. But no agreement was reached over Tangier. The French argued that its "special character" could be preserved only by leaving it under the direct authority of the Sultan. Since the Sultan could now act only through the French Resident General, Tangier would in this way pass under French control. The British insisted on "internationalization," a new and vague idea; what they meant by it was some arrangement by which France could be supervised and out-voted by England and Spain.

In August 1914 the French applied their interpretation to Tangier by treating it as part of the French zone and expelling the diplomatic representatives of the Central Powers. Great Britain countered by refusing to recognize the French protectorate in Morocco. The deadlock was not resolved until 1923. Then the French had the Ruhr conflict on their hands and were anxious to get other difficulties with England out of the way. Therefore they at last offered to England and Spain an acceptable compromise—the Tangier Statute. The statute did not allay British suspicions: it put Tangier under the joint control of England, France and Spain, but it added the Sultan's representative as a fourth, and he was, in British eyes, a French dependent. To make sure of an anti-French majority a further Power had to be brought in; and therefore Fascist Italy was stirred up to voice her claims as a Mediterranean Power. In 1928 the French agreed to revise the statute and to add Italy to the governing Powers.

The system of the statute was a strange tangle. In origin and in essence it was a condominium of the four Powers who made it: France genuinely concerned with the welfare of Tangier (as of the rest of Morocco); England, Spain and Italy engaged solely in thwarting the French plans. But Tangier was still part of Morocco; and the Sultan's representative

counted for much with the Moorish population, in spite of
his subordination to the French—in fact, Tangier was the
only part of Morocco still administered by Moorish officials
and with a Moorish police. Finally, representatives of the
smaller Powers were included on the governing council and
allowed to concern themselves with the drainage in order to
give a spurious international air to the scheme. In reality it
was not international, but an elaborate make-believe by
which England and her two Mediterranean dependents,
Italy and Spain, prevented Tangier from falling into French
hands, a make-believe which became nonsensical and dangerous when it turned out that Italy and Spain were dependents
not of England but of Germany.

The original statute was to last for twelve years. It ran
out in 1935 and, since the Abyssinian crisis was no moment
to denounce it, was automatically renewed until 1947. But
it died before its time. Italy lost her rights by going to war
in 1940, Spain by acting against the statute: in June 1940
Spanish troops entered Tangier, and later in the year Spain
professed to incorporate Tangier in the Spanish zone. Moreover, the statute was a private arrangement between the four
Powers who made it, not the work of an international conference. Particularly it has never been recognized by the United
States, which, as a party to the Algeciras Conference of
1906 on Morocco, still treats the Sultan of Morocco as an
independent ruler. England and France are still bound to
each other by the agreement of 1904, with its subsequent
modifications, but they are not bound to either Spain or
Italy. The question of Tangier, and indeed of the Spanish
zone as well, has to be approached afresh, and the British
Foreign Office will have to discover some principle more
constructive than that of keeping the French out of Tangier.
It might even try the experiment of acting in the spirit,
instead of on the letter, of the Entente Cordiale.

XV

TWO PRIME MINISTERS

(1) *Lord John Russell*

LORD JOHN RUSSELL as Prime Minister, leading and inspiring a government, was not a success: indeed, his government of 1846 to 1852 was the ruin of the Whig party; it never composed a government again, and his government of 1865 to 1866, which might be described as the first Liberal government, was very nearly the ruin of the Liberal party too. He was certainly not a great leader: he was not "outsize" —I do not mean in stature, though he was tiny; I mean in character. He was not more than life-size as really great political figures are—Gladstone, for instance. He spoke aridly, with a dry pedantic voice, and made no effort to win the affection of his followers. He was the first Prime Minister not to take direct personal responsibility for the public finances; and the finances of his government (it was their worst feature) were always rickety—like those of a spendthrift Whig peer. He was too sensitive, too, to be a successful politician, so upset by the criticisms of his diplomatic muddles during the Crimean War that he had to take to buying land as a distraction. He had too much pride to get on with his fellows: pride of the House of Russell, of being a son of the sixth Duke of Bedford, pride, also, at having a better intellect and a better education than most politicians. Still, these are both things worth being proud of, and they are the things which give Russell his place in history.

His life spanned the change from aristocratic to middle-class England, from the England of broad acres to the England of factory chimneys. Russell was the man of the transition, the link between the old order and the new; belonging to the old order by birth, carried over to the new order by his ideas. He was the last great Whig; he became the first Liberal.

Russell, more than any other single man, created the Victorian compromise; he made the England that we know, or knew rather, the England that is vanishing before our eyes.

The unique thing in our political history is the way that we have been able to carry through great changes without violent revolution, going fast enough (just) to satisfy rising social classes without driving the possessing classes into open resistance. Someone has just ascertained that a third of the members of the present House of Commons are the sons of manual labourers; a little more than a hundred years ago five Members of Parliament out of six were landowners—that is the measure of our revolution. The symbol of that revolution was the Reform of Parliament in 1832. The Reform Bill does not look much in itself: the vote was still limited to quite a small electorate, and the House of Commons remained much as it had been before—in fact, for some years, there were rather more aristocrats and landowners in it. But the Reform Bill was a promise, it was a guarantee that the Constitution would not be treated as something rigid and fixed for ever, but as a set of habits which would change as public opinion changed. The Reform Bill was not intended to prepare the way for democracy; indeed, its purpose was to win over the prosperous middle classes to the side of the governing order and so bar the way against democracy, the rule of the people. Russell, its principal architect, defended it for years as a final settlement and opposed, for instance, the radical demands of the Chartists. All the same, it was the vital and decisive concession which set the pattern for the political changes which have followed. Russell himself, in 1866, at the end of his political life, started the discussions for the second Reform Bill, which granted universal suffrage, or as good as maybe, in the towns—and so accepted the principle of democracy.

I have called Russell the principal architect of the Reform Bill. That is true in the sense that, although a junior minister without a seat in the Cabinet, he was one of the three who drafted the original bill in 1831, and also in the sense that he was chosen to introduce the Bill into the House of Commons. It is true in a deeper sense that Russell, more than any other, represented the willingness of the great Whig families to surrender their position of privilege in the State. No, that is wrong: they thought that the more they surrendered of their legal privileges the more their claim to political pre-eminence would be recognized. Russell himself never forgot that he was a member of one of the greatest ducal families and, I dare say, ranked the House of Russell higher than most royalty. When, as a young man, he visited Napoleon on the Island of Elba, they discussed these topics in order of their importance; the political influence of the Duke of Bedford; the allowance which the Duke paid to his son; and third, the condition of France and Italy. Despite his own intellectual ability, he never supposed that ability was a qualification for office— look at the colleagues he chose for his government in 1846. Long after the Reform Bill, Russell never imagined that high office would cease to be a monopoly of the Russells and Cavendishes and Stanleys, the "Venetian oligarchy" which Disraeli wrongly supposed to have existed in the eighteenth century, but which really existed in the early reign of Victoria.

All the same, and this was his redeeming quality, Russell believed in liberty. No doubt he regarded this, too, as a sort of family property. He never forgot that Lord William Russell, who was the founder of the family greatness and whose life he wrote, had died on the scaffold for conspiring against Charles II; for the sake of this ancestor, Russell, too, had to be on the side of radicals and rebels. The ideas of the Glorious Revolution of 1688 were still to Russell living ideas; and the guiding idea of 1688 was certainly liberty. Liberty meant then—and often still meant to Russell —the liberty of the property-owner to do what he liked with his property; but it had been justified by appealing to the will of the people and, therefore, when a popular cause arose, Russell, despite his whiggish narrowness, had to come down on the popular side. Russell took the lead in turning the Whigs into political reformers. The results of these reforms, as we see them to-day, would often have surprised him. But if you ask why there are still dukes, why there is still a House of Lords and why we still listen, sometimes with respect and always with patience, to the opinions of members

H

of the House of Russell, the answer is: Lord John Russell
and his devotion, in his own phrase, to "the cause of civil and
religious liberty all over the world."

Russell led the Whigs in their conversion to reform; he
was not, though, the only reformer among the Whigs. In a
different sphere of public affairs he took the lead more on
his own: he was, I think, the link, and the only one, between
the governing classes and the new economic idea of individualism, of *laissez faire*. Two tremendous changes took
place in England in Russell's lifetime. One was the political
change. The other was a change in economic outlook, which
cleared the way for the fabulous prosperity of this country
later in the nineteenth century: the change from the traditional
pattern of life in which every man had his allotted place in
society:

> The rich man in his castle
> The poor man at his gate
> He made them high and lowly
> And ordered their estate,

a society in which even the poorest had some sort of assured
existence, the change from this to the view that men were
"hands," that their labour was a commodity, the price of
which (like any other commodity) should be determined by
the law of supply and demand. This was the great revolutionary discovery of the early nineteenth century: that there
were so-called natural economic laws (actually extremely
unnatural) and that the only job of government was to get
out of the way and let these laws work. Everything, even
human beings, had to be subordinated to the "price
mechanism," that terrible Moloch to which old-fashioned
economists still bow down. We do not care for the "law of
the market" now that it has become the "American way of
life"; it looks too much like the law of the jungle. But in its
day it was a tremendous instrument of progress. In fact, as a
result of it, human productivity increased more in a century
than in all the rest of recorded history.

It is easy to trace the growth of these new ideas in writers
and thinkers, not so easy to see how they were translated
into practice. It is a bigger question than merely Free Trade

—the part of the change which Peel came to understand. It was the transformation of the whole of social life. Russell was the only member of the ruling classes, the only man in really high office, who understood what Bentham and the economists were driving at. He had been educated: instead of going to Cambridge, where he might have learnt a little mathematics (and that would have done his finances, private and public, no harm), or to Oxford where he could have learnt only theology and classics, the two most useless studies known to men—instead he went to Edinburgh and learnt economics and political theory.

Later in life he was a friend of Nassau Senior, the leading orthodox economist of the day, and swallowed his doctrines open-mouthed, as recently our rulers tried to keep up with every flash of Keynes's nimble brain. Therefore it was no accident that Russell introduced the new Poor Law in 1834, the most revolutionary economic measure of the early nineteenth century. The new Poor Law swept away the old principle of the right to work or maintenance, the idea that society had some responsibility for its members; it substituted the idea that men must be driven to work by hunger—the basic idea without which capitalism will not work. We are trying to work capitalism without it now; hence all our present troubles. The new Poor Law and all that it implied—treating human beings as individuals who must struggle for themselves or else succumb—all this was Russell's work. He showed this in his attitude to the Irish Famine of 1847, which took place when he was Prime Minister. Russell was a tender-hearted man and was made wretched by the thought of all the suffering of the Irish; but he set his face against any measure of relief which would interfere with the workings of natural economic law. He was the man who translated the theories of the economists into practice.

Russell himself would have added other claims to fame. He attached great importance to his fight for religious freedom, by which he meant, to put it crudely, keeping the churches in their place, a very subordinate place. His own religion was a vague benevolent Deism and he had no patience with deep religious feelings. He made a famous reply to a

Dean of Hereford who had scruples against electing as Bishop someone whom Russell had nominated: "Dear Sir, I have received your letter in which you inform me of your intention to break the law." The most popular act of his life was not the Reform Bill, but the Ecclesiastical Titles Bill of 1851, which forbade Roman Catholic bishops to take territorial titles of places in England—an odd way of defending religious liberty. Even odder, the last public act of this soldier of liberty was to congratulate Bismarck for his campaign against the Roman Catholic Church in Germany. In fact Russell was a Protestant, in the sense of being hostile to the Church of Rome, but not a Christian; a combination formerly common, though now, I think, extinct.

Russell was proud, too, of his record as Foreign Secretary between 1859 and 1865, when Palmerston was Prime Minister. He had objected to Palmerston's wildness, when he had been Prime Minister and Palmerston Foreign Secretary; but, curiously enough, Russell was much wilder when the roles were reversed. Russell's stock-in-trade as Foreign Secretary was the hectoring lecturing dispatch, when he told foreign rulers the awful things that would happen to them if they did not follow the British constitutional pattern. He lectured the Tsar on how to govern Poland; he lectured the Emperor of Austria on the way to treat Hungary; he lectured Bismarck for daring to attack Denmark; he lectured the United States for having a civil war; he lectured the whole of Europe on the virtues of Italian Nationalism. In fact he started the tradition that it is part of the duty of a British Foreign Secretary to tell other countries how to run their affairs. Russell never followed up his lectures with any kind of action; he thought it would be quite enough to threaten Tsars and Emperors with his displeasure, the displeasure of a member of the House of Russell. He only succeeded in bringing the name of Great Britain into contempt. Still, if only these rulers had listened, Russell, in his pedantic way, had something to tell them: this country had hit on the secret of making great social and political changes without revolution, and it was Russell who had shown how the trick was done.

(2) *Lord Salisbury*

Lord Salisbury was a consistent Tory. He never wavered in his principles and never deserted them: in 1867 he risked his political future rather than agree to the democratic Reform Bill with which Derby and Disraeli hoped to "dish the Whigs," and twenty years later he took office as the uncompromising opponent of Home Rule. He came off one of the few genuinely Tory families—and one of the few, too, which went back beyond the Glorious Revolution, a family which had never joined in the hunt for honours under the Hanoverians. Two great Cecils, William and Robert, had served Elizabeth and James I, then came an unbroken row of nonentities for more than two hundred years. Here is the strange thing about Salisbury: he was distinguished from his ancestors by his intellectual gifts, which were very great: he had the political and religious outlook of a slow-witted countryman. His own thinking was ruthless—he spared nothing and nobody; the political creed to which he held had been hammered out by generations of Englishmen who distrusted thought in politics. He hated society and social functions, he was impatient with hereditary distinctions; the party which he led existed to preserve the social order and valued hereditary claims. He arrived at his own conclusions by private thought, locked away in his study behind double doors, never consulting others until his mind was fully made up; yet he spoke with contempt of the study-made conclusions of political thinkers. His followers cared for the English countryside and for country pursuits; he disliked horses and preferred the villa which he built at Dieppe to his historic house at Hatfield. The Tory party has been called the stupid party (and not unfairly, to be stupid and to be sensible are not far apart. The Progressive party, radical and socialist, is clever, but silly). Strange indeed: the most successful leader that the stupid party has had since the Reform Bill was an intellectual, supremely clever.

This contrast gives Salisbury's character a special fascination. Most Prime Ministers would not be interesting unless they had been Prime Ministers (and some are not interesting even then): most of their biographies are heavy going even for the historian—think of the dead-weight of Morley's *Gladstone*, or Monypenny and Buckle on Disraeli. But Lady Gwendolen Cecil's life of her father is a work of art, a great biography which can be read for pleasure by someone with no interest in political history at all. Salisbury would have been a remarkable man even if he had never been Prime Minister or even if he had never gone into politics at all. He was a character as Dr. Johnson was a character, and on the same scale. Think of his monumental absent-mindedness which led him to greet his own son, encountered in the grounds of Hatfield House, as an important but unrecognized guest. Once at a breakfast party, sitting on his host's left, he asked in an undertone who was the distinguished man on the host's right. It was Mr. W. H. Smith, Salisbury's Chancellor of the Exchequer, who had sat at Salisbury's side in Cabinet for years. Equally delightful was his scientific enthusiasm, which led him to put glaring and erratic electric light into Hatfield House: it worked from the river and sank to a dull red when the stream was low. Hatfield was also wired for a primitive telephone, with a sort of loud-speaker attachment, by means of which Salisbury could boom into every room: "Hey diddle diddle, the cat and the fiddle; the cow jumped over the moon."

He was a first-rate writer. His letters and dispatches are still, after half a century, a delight to read—no one could say the same of Peel or even of Gladstone. His political journalism is as fresh now as when it was written. His essay on the Polish question, for instance, written in 1863, is the most sensible thing ever written on Poland and Russia: it was heavily drawn on by Mr. Eden during the debate in the House of Commons which followed the Yalta Agreement of 1945. Only Mr. Eden jibbed at the conclusion that the best one can hope for Poland is that she should enjoy a limited autonomy under Russian protection. He was a master of the telling phrase. "Backing the wrong horse"—the policy of propping up Turkey instead of co-operating with Russia in the Near East. "Splendid isolation"—not, as is often supposed, a description of his policy, but a reminder that only a Power whose vital interests are not involved can examine a problem in an "emotional and philanthropic spirit." Some of his most telling phrases had a jaunty air which would have brought the wrath of Mr. Ensor and the Lord President of the Council down on me if I had used them. Thus he described the Cape-to-Cairo railway as "a curious idea which has lately become prevalent"; and the conflict of the Great Powers in China as "a sort of diplomatic cracker that has produced a great many detonations, but I think the smoke of it has now floated into the distance." When the Russians occupied Port Arthur in 1898 he wrote that the British public will demand "some territorial or cartographic consolation in China. It will not be useful, and it will be expensive; but as a matter of pure sentiment, we shall have to do it." Once, defending an agreement which assigned to France a large part of the Sahara, he said: "This is what agriculturists would call very 'light' land"—not a tactful way of recommending the agreement to French public opinion.

All these dazzling phrases are about foreign affairs, and foreign policy was his consuming interest. He first stepped into the front rank in politics in 1878; he became Foreign Secretary in place of Lord Derby and got British foreign policy out of the mess into which it had been landed by the conflict between the pacifism of Derby and the erratic, unpredictable bellicosity of Disraeli. Sitting in the House of Lords—he was the last Prime Minister to sit in the Lords and I don't suppose we shall have another, the peerage is not likely to produce a man of Salisbury's genius in centuries—he had few parliamentary cares and, except for a few months in 1886 and again for a few months at the end of his life, he combined the jobs of Prime Minister and Foreign Secretary. He was very much the senior, too, in his Cabinets. He could conduct foreign policy, virtually uncontrolled—not checked by a Prime Minister, not interfered with much by the Cabinet, and remote even from questions in the House of Commons. Add to this that Rosebery, the Liberal Foreign Secretary in the short break between Salisbury's governments, was virtually imposed on Gladstone by the Queen, at Salisbury's prompting, and that Rosebery was Salisbury's obedient pupil. As a result, Salisbury had fifteen years, from 1885 to 1900, of directing foreign policy, a record in our history; and, moreover, it was really a policy he directed. He was fond of saying that a British Foreign Secretary could have no policy. In his own words "British policy is to drift lazily downstream, occasionally putting out a boat-hook to avoid a collision." But this apparent planlessness was really a device to keep his hands free and to conceal his plans from foreigners. There is nothing in the history of our foreign policy to compare with the prolonged and patient way in which Salisbury solved the difficulties of the British position in Egypt, isolating Egypt first from one country and then another, and finally staging the open challenge to France at Fashoda in 1898. Indeed, I would say that Salisbury laid down the lines on which British foreign policy was to develop for many years after his death: he saw that so long as we were quarrelling with France and Russia all over the world—in Egypt, in Persia, in the Far East— we were dependent on German favour, and he was determined to escape this favour. Therefore, slowly and persistently, he prepared the way for the Anglo-French entente, which matured in 1904, and the Anglo-Russian entente, which matured in 1907. At the very basis of his thought was the fact that has been brought home to us by two great wars: if England and Russia, the two Great Powers on the edge of Europe, fall out, they will have Europe, in the shape of Germany, on their backs. That is why Salisbury, greatest of our Foreign Secretaries, was the greatest advocate of Anglo-Russian co-operation.

In comparison with these great world affairs, Salisbury had less interest in the humdrum tasks of a Prime Minister. He was too outspoken to be a good manager of men and could never have been a successful leader of the House of Commons. But, to his surprise, he found that he could compete with Gladstone as a public speaker at mass meetings: like many intellectuals, an impersonal mass audience drew him out where a few dozen individuals did not. He spoke in the fine Victorian way without notes, sometimes pausing for as much as thirty seconds between sentences; the effect was ponderous, absolutely sincere, like the strokes of a great hammer. But, with this sincerity and greatness of character, what had he to say? Very little. The only question on which he felt strongly was the defence of the Established Church. This marks him off from other Victorian Prime Ministers: most of them were lukewarm in religion. Gladstone, on the other hand, was so devout that he desired to disestablish the Church so that it could develop the virtue of apostolic poverty. Apart from this, Salisbury excelled at exposing the follies of others, but had little to advocate himself. Though a good landlord in private life, he had no social philosophy: he accepted private enterprise and Free Trade like any Liberal. When Disraeli urged that the Conservatives ought to take the lead in social reform, Salisbury complained that Disraeli was "feather-brained."

The truth is that this great man, so free from illusions, had one great illusion: fear of democracy and belief in the virtue of resisting for resisting's sake. During the American Civil War, when he was, of course, strongly on the side of the slave-owning South, his mind was so agitated that he took to sleep-walking, and one night his wife saw him rise from his bed and stand at the open window, warding off an imaginary attack; it was the forces of democracy trying to break into Hatfield House. He spoke all his life as though democracy was a sort of germ people catch, much as people now talk of Communism as a germ that will get into the Western world unless we keep the Greek window closed. Instead of the process of compromise between parties which has been the normal pattern of our political life, he wanted to make a sharp division between them and to have a fight. The issue he found to fight on was Irish Home Rule. Gladstone had hoped that the Conservatives would carry Home Rule, as Peel had carried Free Trade. Instead Salisbury—it was his decision that mattered—made it the matter of political conflict for a generation. In one sense it did the trick: it gave the Conservatives almost twenty years of office. But at a high price. It left the Irish question to be settled later at a terrible cost in bitterness and bloodshed. It taught the Conservatives to value violence and pugnacity as a policy and so led them to the follies of defending the House of Lords in 1910 and to the worse-than-folly of the Ulster rebellion in 1914. What is more, it made

Salisbury himself the prisoner of all the violent men prepared to resist Home Rule, the prisoner of Joseph Chamberlain and of the unscrupulous Imperialists, the prisoner even of Cecil Rhodes.

Salisbury had begun as the leader of devout country gentlemen with centuries of honest tradition behind them. He ended as the leader of the Unionists, the party of the City and of high finance. He took the lead in the partition in Africa in order to end the slave trade; this was not the motive of his party-backers in the Chartered Companies. His last great act was to lead this country into the Boer War. Undoubtedly he hoped to establish the British ideal of racial equality in South Africa. The Boer War made the gold and diamonds secure for the city companies; it has not, so far, benefited the South African native. And here, I think, we have got to the secret of his strange personality, of the contrast between his private charitableness and the bitterness of his public expression: he loved the joy of battle, but found no worthy cause for which to fight. He fought for victory; he expected defeat. His two great ancestors had founded the greatness of the British Empire; Salisbury heard from afar the notes which announced its end. When Salisbury resigned in 1902, old England too passed from the stage of history.

PART TWO

CONTEMPORARY

I

M. FLANDIN AND FRENCH POLICY

M. FLANDIN, one-time Prime Minister, is the latest French politician to essay a defence of his pre-war policy; in this case defence is literal, for the book[1] was written while M. Flandin was in prison in Algiers after the Allied landing. The defence is disguised as a history of French foreign policy between the wars; this records the errors of others, often with justification. However, one hardly need trouble about M. Flandin as an historian; the useful part of the book is the personal reminiscences. These concern Stresa, when he was Prime Minister, and the reoccupation of the Rhineland, when he was Foreign Minister. M. Flandin became Prime Minister in November 1934. His aim, he explains, was to restore good relations with England and Italy, and, at the same time, to develop the entente with Russia which Barthou had begun; here he claims to have imposed the Franco-Soviet Pact on Laval, his Foreign Minister. His purpose in keeping Laval as Foreign Minister, he adds, was "to shelter under Laval's policy of Franco-German reconciliation, which secured me against attacks from the G rmanophil Anglo-Saxon superpacifists." Thus it was really British public opinion which kept Laval in office! M. Flandin claims, too, that he secured a military convention with Italy, but that this was resisted by Laval, in order not to offend German feelings.

On Abyssinia, Flandin claims to have warned Mussolini (through Ciano) not to act without British approval; Ciano answered that there would be no difficulties on the British side. This view was based on the silence of MacDonald and Sir John Simon at the Stresa meeting, when Mussolini had hinted at African questions without provoking a response. Flandin was out of office during the height of the Abyssinian

[1] *Politique Française*, 1919–1940. By Pierre-Etienne Flandin.

crisis. In April 1936, as Foreign Minister, he proposed to
Mr. Eden a compromise which would have preserved some
part of Abyssinia for the Emperor. Mr. Eden is alleged to
have replied that rapid Italian success was not likely: "Not
only will they not be in Addis Ababa in a few weeks, but the
rainy season will soon begin, which will give the Negus time
and possibility to reinforce his army, and, when we meet
here in September for the Assembly, believe me, Mussolini's
claims will be much lower." The Italian armies entered
Addis Ababa early in May.

The reoccupation of the Rhineland was the turning-point
of French policy, as it is of this book. In January 1936 Flandin
asked the British Government what it would do in case of a
German violation of the neutralization of the Rhineland.
Baldwin answered: What has the French Government decided
to do? It had decided nothing; and Flandin returned to Paris
to attempt to extract a decision from his Government. All he
got was a declaration of French readiness "to place at the
disposal of the League of Nations her military, naval and air
forces, to oppose by force a violation of the Treaties." Nothing
was, in fact, decided, when the Germans acted on March 7.
In the French Cabinet the Minister of War declared that, in
order to intervene in the Rhineland, general mobilization
was necessary.

With the elections six weeks off, this was judged impossible; and only four Ministers—Sarraut, the Prime
Minister, Mandel, Paul-Boncour, and Flandin—favoured
immediate action. Instead, France waited for the meeting of
the Locarno Powers; these merely referred the question to
the Council of the League and—again according to Flandin
—Mr. Eden argued that the German entry into the Rhineland
was "simply a symbolic act." Finally came the meeting of the
Council in London, when France was opposed by every
member except Mr. Litvinov, "who supported me throughout
by speech and vote." M. Flandin has a special word of bitterness for Beck, who, he alleges, certainly offered to fight side
by side with France against Germany, but refused to confirm
the breach of Locarno on the ground that it did not concern
Poland. Since Flandin was to argue three years later that

Poland did not concern France, he had somehow to argue away the indisputable offer of help from Poland in 1936.

Flandin finally abandoned all hope of action after an interview with Baldwin. Flandin explained that France did not want to drag Great Britain into war.

She will bear alone all the costs and risks of the operation, which will be a simple police affair. All that we ask is that you should let us act. But he replied repeatedly: "Great Britain cannot run the risk of war." And as I disputed this risk he replied: "You may be right; but, even if there is only one chance in a hundred of war coming from your police operation, I have not the right to involve England; because"—and his hesitation showed what it cost him to admit this—"England is not in a condition to make war."

Action on the Rhine after this, Flandin argues, would have involved a breach with Great Britain; instead he emerged from the crisis with a precise Anglo-French Alliance. This tactic was, of course, repeated in the guarantee given to Czechoslovakia after Munich; in both cases the Powers pledged themselves to action only after action had become impossible.

Flandin left office in 1936 and did not return to it. His comments on later events are therefore those of an outsider. He is at pains to insist that the Anschluss was popular in Austria; that France was not pledged to support Czechoslovakia; and that, in any case, there was never a crisis in 1938, since Czechoslovakia did not appeal to the League of Nations. Similarly he argues that France was not committed to Poland in 1939 and that she should have waited for war until her military position had improved. Flandin adds some interesting details on the French declaration of war. On August 27, 1939, he went to Daladier to urge him not to go to war. Daladier argued that Poland was France's last ally in the East; without Poland there could be no second front. Gamelin, too, was optimistic of Polish chances: "The soldiers are excellent and the Command up to its job. The Poles will hold and will give us plenty of time to go to their help . . . they will hold at least six months and we shall go to help them through Rumania." Finally, Flandin claims that on September 2 the Chamber was persuaded into voting credits without debate by the argument that discussion would interfere with the success of Italian mediation; Daladier was allowed to make a resolute speech, with unanimous support, for the sake of a second Munich. British and Polish obstinacy defeated this manœuvre; and France was tricked into war.

It would be a mistake to take M. Flandin at his own valuation as a statesman, or even as a witness. For instance, his account of the events of 1936 does not square with that given by General Gamelin, who, naturally, is concerned to stress the hesitations of the civilians. Still, Flandin's book confirms what we know from other sources: there was no one in France with the character or courage to give a resolute lead, and the disaster of 1940 condemned an entire generation of politicians and soldiers. Of this generation M. Flandin was one.

II

MUNICH TEN YEARS AFTER

THE crisis of Munich has few mysteries for the historian. We know as much about it as about, say, Agadir or the affair of the Hohenzollern candidate which preceded the Franco-German war of 1870. We know, for instance, that Hitler intended all along to destroy Czechoslovakia and that the Sudeten grievances were humbug; we know that Chamberlain's policy of appeasement was sincerely held and deliberately conducted, and that the argument of British weakness was an excuse invented after the event; we know why the French did not fight, even though the French military advisers thought themselves in a better position to fight in 1938 than in 1939; we even know why the Czechs did not fight; we know what the Russians offered (though not their fighting quality). In short, we know—as much as a historian ever knows—the record of facts; and doubt is cast on this record only by those who want to cover something shameful in their own past. There we arrive at what we do not know—why Munich should have such psychological symbolism; why it should still rouse such passion and lead honourable men to lie and cheat about it; why, indeed, it touched off in the House of Commons a scene of "mass-hysteria" without parallel in history. Incidentally here is one of the few points of detail we do not know—who among the Members of Parliament remained silent when all the rest were screaming and sobbing. One observer says Eden and Harold Nicolson; another speaks of Churchill, Eden, and Amery. Both, revealingly, omit Gallacher.

At Munich, for the last time, Europe seemed the centre of the world. As in the fifth act of a Shakespearean tragedy, the characters made a final proud appearance, unwitting that the hand of death was already upon them. The Munich Conference was the last version of the Concert of Europe and, thus, the heir of the Congress of Vienna. It was a meeting

I

of Empires. The British Empire, *l'Empire français*, *Deutsches Reich*—these had been names of confident power. Even Mussolini brandished Imperial phrases and echoed the great claims of Rome. The Munich figures genuinely supposed that they were the "Big Four" on whom depended the peace and security of the world. Yet at the back of their minds all, even Hitler, were haunted by the fear that greatness was passing them by. These rulers of Empires buried themselves in the details of Czech frontier adjustments so as not to lift their eyes and see the writing on the wall. Still, the most gloomy or clear-sighted observer could not have foretold that within ten years only one of the four Munich Powers would be numbered, though with some doubt, among the Great; and even this one is a pensioner of an extra-European Power.

Both the United States and the Soviet Union were absent from Munich, deliberately excluded by the self-confident spokesmen of "Europe." Though Roosevelt was no doubt restrained by the immaturity of American public opinion, Chamberlain, as we now know, had set his face against American participation in the interests of appeasement. Munich rested on the assumption that America was not a Great Power and would never become one. Still more, Munich rounded off twenty years of pretending that Russia did not exist. The Anglo-French wars of intervention between 1917 and 1920, undertaken against a former ally, were the worst international crimes of the century; for they fed the Bolshevik belief that there was inescapable hostility between capitalism and Communism. In the nineteen-thirties this belief weakened a little, and the Russians—lacking other means of defence against Germany—perhaps took seriously the principles which the Western Powers professed. If ever there was a chance of bringing Russia back into the European order on a basis of international morality, that chance was lost at Munich—probably for ever. Russia alone had remained faithful to the idea of collective security; and was made to look foolish for her pains. Later it became fashionable to argue that Russia, too, had been cheating like all the rest. At the time the "men of Munich" were more honest; they did not want Russia in Europe and prided themselves on having kept her out

Anti-Bolshevism, no doubt, strengthened this attitude and gave the relief its hysterical note; still, it was not the main motive—after all, they were just as pleased to have excluded America.

Insistence on Europe to the exclusion of the rest of the world led England and France to inevitable defeat. Munich was the penalty exacted for a misreading of history—the illusion that France and even England were the victors in the first German war. Yet France would have been defeated in 1914 without Russia; England could not have carried the war to final victory without America. But though Munich became a term of reproach in both France and England, it signified different things in the two countries. To the French it meant a conscious retreat from greatness; France gave up the fruits of the victory of 1918 and abandoned her allies in eastern Europe. The French "men of Munich" were traitors to French greatness and, from Daladier downwards, themselves admitted it. They justified their betrayal by arguing that the price of greatness was too high in blood and social upheaval. The French path ran straight from Munich to Vichy; and, after Munich, collaboration alone made sense. Frenchmen who turned against Munich were demanding revolution. This was obvious in the Communists; but Jacobinism—the course of Clemenceau or of de Gaulle—was an equal threat to the Third, as it is to the Fourth Republic. In 1938 the Radicals accepted Munich to preserve the Republic; and to-day, for the same reason, they acquiesce unwillingly in European plans which will again put France in the shadow of German economic power.

In 1938 some Englishmen, too, used the arguments of declining greatness and of the Balance of Power. These arguments still had a harsh, alien ring. Significantly, Duff Cooper, the only Minister to resign, was spiritually at home in France and had written a distinguished book on the greatest of French diplomats. For most Englishmen Munich was a moral issue, not a question of power. One must be just even to the English "men of Munich": they genuinely believed that what they had done was appeasement, not capitulation. Fear of war—for the whole world, not merely for themselves—was, no doubt, the prime motive; and, besides, they could argue that they could not aid the Czechs effectively. The same argument, even better founded, seemed irrelevant a year later, and the English people would have given ineffective aid to the Czechs, as they did to the Poles, if they had been morally prepared against Germany. As it was, they felt the moral strength of the German case. For twenty years, English writers, particularly on the Left, had denounced the injustice of the Versailles settlement and the narrow Nationalism of the Succession States. English and American historians, of irreproachable liberalism, had declared that Germany was no more responsible than any other Power for the war of 1914. Who among us can claim innocence? I, for one, look back with shame to the university lectures on the origins of the war of 1914 which I gave before the German occupation of the Rhineland brought me to my senses.

Liberal opinion had accepted the national principle ever since the creation of national Italy in 1860; and the partition of Czechoslovakia seemed the last victory of nationalism. Moreover, the Czechs were, in some sort, the victims of the propaganda in favour of collective security. Englishmen had had it dinned into them for years that peace was indivisible and that they ought to resist aggression anywhere and everywhere. This appeal for a universal crusade asked too much of ordinary Englishmen; what is more, it led them to regard all resistance to aggression as abstract "idealism." They felt that, except as vindication of a theoretical principle, it did not matter whether the Italians ruled in Addis Ababa—or, for that matter, the Abyssinians in Rome. From this sound conclusion they proceeded to the unsound conclusion that equally it did not matter whether Hitler or Benes ruled in Prague. On the other hand, the teachings of collective security, though ineffective for action, made them ashamed to fight for "selfish" national interests and for the Balance of Power. Englishmen lacked a clear moral cause; and we, the clerks in Julien Benda's phrase, were the real "guilty men" of Munich in that we had failed to provide it.

The Czechs, too, were hampered by their moral position. The Czech leaders, Benes most of all, were liberals by historical background and social origin—men of bargaining and discussion. They could manœuvre and evade; they could not defy and perish. Without the long series of Czech concessions and offers to the Germans Munich would not have been possible; and the Munich Conference was the last display of liberal civilization. Reason and negotiation were ineffective against German power; the only answer was cannon, the *ultima ratio regis*. Benes could not bring himself to make this answer; it was given by Colonel Beck, a man of infinitely lower moral calibre, but all the same the man who gave the signal for Hitler's fall.

As it was, Munich seemed to bring Hitler triumph; and he deserved it. The other "men of Munich" were all, in their way, playing old parts and trying to dodge reality; they dreamt of a pacific Europe without conflicts of power. Hitler took Munich seriously and supposed that the others did so too. If Europe was to stand alone without either Russia or America, then Germany, as the only Great Power in Europe, must dominate it. The Europe of equal and independent states was finished, blighted by the chimneys of the Ruhr. If Munich did not mean this, then it had no sense.

The former "men of Munich" in this country now parade their conversion: the greater the readiness to conciliate Hitler ten years ago, the more determined the resolve to resist the Russians now. The argument from experience is trivial and was indeed proved wrong by Munich itself. "Appeasement" of France over the Belgian question proved successful in the eighteen-thirties; therefore it was supposed that it would prove successful with Germany over the Czech question in the nineteen-thirties. What will prove successful with the Russians has to be decided by serious political analysis, not by such twaddling scraps of history. In any case appeasement or resistance was not the fundamental issue of Munich. The fundamental issue of Munich was whether England (or more generally the Western Powers) could work with Russia in order to give all Europe—including Germany—a settled existence. Thus, at bottom, the "men of Munich" are being true to themselves when they lick their lips over the prospect of a conflict which will expel Russia from Europe and so restore the European circumstances of October 1938.

III

THE DIPLOMACY OF M. BONNET

M. BONNET, French Foreign Minister in 1938 and 1939, feels himself, perhaps with some reason, the scapegoat for Munich; he was the "fall guy." Daladier was vindicated in the French parliament; Neville Chamberlain was eulogized by Churchill after his death; Lord Halifax served the Coalition and Labour governments as ambassador at Washington. Only M. Bonnet is reduced to defending himself. His first volume runs from his appointment as Foreign Minister until the end of the Munich crisis; the second from Munich to the outbreak of war.[1] This book will certainly serve to acquit Bonnet of one charge. Superficial, fatuous, self-satisfied, the author of these memoirs could never have been a cynical, far-sighted plotter, engineering the destruction of Czechoslovakia or organizing a European coalition against the Soviet Union.

The book seems almost to have been written by two different hands. One Bonnet, rambling and diffuse, gives a rehash of the old Munichite stock-in-trade or, as he calls it, "the philosophy of the crisis." France was too weak to fight; alternatively she would have fought if she had not been prevented by the unwillingness of her allies, including the Czechs. Munich was a device for buying time; alternatively, it was a just revision of the settlement of 1919, a victory for the principle of self-determination. France was unable to help Czechoslovakia; alternatively, by obtaining a British guarantee for post-Munich Czechoslovakia, France made Czechslovakia stronger than before. Most of all, war would destroy "all that gave a value to life." No more Radical-Socialist party! No more Third Republic! In truth, the French and British ministers were resolved from the beginning to do

[1] Volume I: *Defense de la Paix. De Washington au Quai d'Orsay.* Volume II: *Fin d'une Europe. De Munich à la Guerre.* By Georges Bonnet.

nothing. Their world was coming to an end, and they had only one aim: to postpone the earthquake for a year, for a month, for a day.

The other Bonnet is a skilled diplomatist or, at any rate, had skilled diplomatists at his service. France, it appears, was attempting to build a grand alliance against Germany; every ally failed her, only France remained true to her obligations. Bonnet's real aim was different. He was convinced that the French system in Europe would collapse at the first touch and was concerned to put the blame on others, to possess written proofs against the allies of France without leaving on paper proofs against himself. With America his task was easy. The United States would do nothing; and when, in September, Bullitt, the American ambassador, expressed a few harmless phrases about Franco-American friendship, he was at once repudiated by Roosevelt. England comes next. The British Government clung obstinately to the basic contradiction of its Locarno policy: it would defend the independence of France, but it would not defend the international order in eastern Europe on which this independence rested. In April 1938 the British Government agreed to "bluff" Hitler: it would give the Czechs diplomatic support in order to prod them into concessions, but it would not go to war. Before 1914 the British Government had also tried to draw a dividing line between the security of France and the state of things in eastern Europe; but then there had been a French Government proud enough to follow an independent line which finally brought England and Russia into the war as allies. In 1938 the French Government dared not act independently; the British refusal left it helpless and at a loss.

British policy, unchanged since 1925, was only one element in the French collapse. The system of alliances in eastern Europe collapsed also. The deepest cause of this collapse was Poland, a country without real strength, which aspired to play the part of a Great Power. The Polish Government would do nothing to help Czechoslovakia, still less would they permit the passage of a Russian army across Polish territory. Instead, they intended to join Hitler in dismembering Czechoslovakia. Bonnet says of his allies:

"We heard only one bellicose voice: that of Poland. But she was thinking of making war on Czechoslovakia!" But who had inflated Poland to give her the appearance of a Great Power? Who had encouraged her to act as a rampart of anti-Bolshevism? A succession of French governments. Bonnet failed to see that the position of Poland as a so-called Great Power. rested on the alliance with France and that a firm French policy must have immediately brought the Poles to reason. Poland could flirt with Germany so long as she had France as an ally; she could never risk being left alone with Germany.

Once Polish hostility has been satisfactorily proved, Bonnet has got past his most awkward moment: the refusal of the Russian efforts at co-operation. The Russians would support Czechoslovakia provided that France did the same; but they would cross Poland or Rumania only with the consent of the government concerned and, since France was the ally of both, it was for France to obtain their consent. This was the reply given by Litvinov on May 12 and repeated by him on September 11. Poland put a veto on Russian action; therefore there was nothing more to be done. Besides, Poland was so strong that she could even forbid the passage of Russian troops across Rumania; and, in any case, the Rumanians feared for Bessarabia—they were glad enough to shelter behind the Polish veto. The Rumanians hinted that their anti-aircraft batteries were too weak to interfere with the flight of Russian planes. Bonnet does not appear to have conveyed this information to the Russians. But, then, it is the essence of his case that the Russians (unlike the French) did not mean their declarations of support for Czechoslovakia to be taken seriously. Thus, with Poland hostile and Russia barred from action, France was helpless.

The final blow was delivered by the Czechs themselves, who shrank from resistance. On September 21, Hodza, the Czech Prime Minister, implored Bonnet to repudiate the Franco-Czech alliance, so that the Czech ministers would be obliged to give way; and Bonnet gave him this "cover." Bonnet is not content with this gesture of self-sacrifice; he seeks to prove his own success and makes much of the British guarantee which was given to Czechoslovakia after Munich. Great Britain and France claimed that because of their military weakness and their geographic position they could do nothing to help Czechoslovakia, when she was fully mobilized and entrenched behind her natural frontiers. They deprived her of these frontiers and of her defensive equipment; they broke her national spirit and obliged her to disarm. And at the same moment they declared themselves capable of protecting her against future danger. It was the worst transaction of a shameful era.

Munich was the collapse of a European system, of a system which tried to give Europe security without asking any military or diplomatic effort from the Great Powers. This system rested on a series of pretences. It assumed that France was the strongest Power in Europe and that Germany had been converted to a peaceful policy; that Russia was not a Great Power and could be permanently excluded from Europe; above all, that the States of eastern Europe could maintain their economic and political independence without assistance. This system was bound to collapse. The problem of the overwhelming power of Germany could not be solved within the limits of the European continent. It could be solved only if Germany, who overshadowed Europe, could be eclipsed in her turn by the three great world Powers, who had tried to turn their backs on Europe. It was hopeless for France to try to maintain this European system alone, as she had done in the years after Versailles. And it was hardly less hopeless to try to maintain it solely with British assistance. A wise French policy would have aimed to win the support of Russia and the United States. With America there was nothing to be done. Alliance with Soviet Russia was the more essential. This was the key to the survival of France as a great, or even as an independent, Power. Instead, the policy of Munich destroyed Russian belief (never very strong) in French determination and so opened the way to the Nazi-Soviet pact. A system of politics was in collapse. Twenty years of taking phrases for reality produced their inevitable result, and the statesmen of every country behaved meanly, feebly. The worst fault was to be complacent, to be proud of their work; this fault, too, Bonnet shared with others.

In the second volume the reader will soon detect the familiar sleight of hand. For instance, in reference to Ribbentrop's visit to Paris in December 1938, there occur the innocent sentences: "He then attended a lunch at which I was not present. Towards the end of the afternoon he was taken to visit the Louvre." Who would guess from this that Bonnet and Ribbentrop passed the afternoon together at the Louvre alone? On the other hand, those who study in detail the written record will be confirmed in the view that M. Bonnet was rather more adroit, and not markedly less scrupulous, than most other Foreign Ministers of the Third Republic.

Bonnet has little to tell concerning the Franco-German declaration of December 6, 1938, by which he was accused later of handing over eastern Europe to Germany. His documents show that he reminded Ribbentrop of the Franco-Polish alliance and of the Franco-Soviet pact, and that Ribbentrop accepted these reservations. No doubt this amounted to little at a time when Poland, after seizing Teschen, seemed on better terms with Germany than with France. The Franco-German declaration assumed a German preponderance in eastern Europe and such "moderate" gains as the recovery of Danzig; but it also assumed that Germany would proceed in a plausible way and would save the faces of French and especially British statesmen. Instead, Hitler seized Prague and made it impossible for Chamberlain and Lord Halifax to continue the line of appeasement, even if they had wished to do so. They needed a symbol of their new resolve; this symbol was the guarantee of Poland.

The guarantee to Poland was a disaster to French policy. Since England had no army, the guarantee was in effect a promise that France would not fail the Poles as she had failed the Czechs. France could not break with England, yet was incapable of helping the Poles. The only solution was to bring in the Soviet Union. Poland had been the decisive obstacle to this at the time of Munich; and the Polish refusal was reaffirmed by Beck on March 26, 1939. M. Bonnet devised a new tactic: he would secure Soviet aid and then threaten to abandon Poland to her fate unless she accepted it—a move which would also perhaps clear France in British eyes. This tactic was explained to the Soviet Ambassador on April 10. France and the Soviet Union, M. Bonnet said, should settle Soviet aid to Rumania and Poland: "We should then have to decide the attitude to take in case either Rumania or Poland refused this aid." But the Soviet rulers were not satisfied with the French alliance which Bonnet offered; the British guarantee to Poland would enable Poland to resist Franco-Soviet pressure and therefore they insisted that Great Britain must be included in the alliance negotiations. Hence the prolonged negotiations from April until July. The Russians demanded an alliance of mutual guarantee and the virtual recognition of the Soviet Union as the preponderant Power in eastern Europe; the British desired a bargain by which the Soviet Union would aid her neighbours only if called upon to do so. The British Government tried to give the impression that England and France were conducting a joint negotiation with the Soviet Union; in reality, as M. Bonnet shows, France was willing from the first to accept the Soviet terms and used every means (including the threat of French impotence) to drag Britain along with her.

French diplomacy succeeded. On July 24 a political agreement was reached which accepted all the Soviet demands —mutual assistance, inclusion of the Baltic countries, freedom to act without a request for assistance from the country attacked, and a wide definition of indirect aggression as "an act accepted by the State in question under threat of force by another Power and involving the abandonment of its independence or of its neutrality." All these demands had been backed by the French with extreme urgency. It was a striking achievement on paper. In practice, England and Russia were probably more suspicious of each other than before, and the agreement was to come into force only when a military convention had been made. Poland's refusal remained the core of the matter.

With Russia the problem had been to reach an agreement; with Poland it was to avoid one. Immediately after the British guarantee to Poland, the Poles asked Bonnet to add to the Franco-Polish alliance a similar guarantee. He agreed, since he was already committed by the British action. The Poles attempted to smuggle in a new clause extending the guarantee to Danzig and alleged that a similar clause was being settled in London. Inquiry in London proved (according to Bonnet's evidence) that this was untrue: the British, like the French, were hanging back until they had settled with the Russians. M. Corbin, the French Ambassador in London, reported on June 5 that the Foreign Office "thought that it could be inconvenient to establish definitively the text of the Anglo-Polish agreement before knowing certainly what form the tripartite treaty with the U.S.S.R. will take." Bonnet hints also that he, at any rate, was still keeping Danzig up his sleeve as a bargaining counter with Germany. The discussions with Poland had, however, an outcome highly inconvenient to Bonnet's policy. To divert the Poles from revising the political terms, Bonnet (and Daladier) proposed staff conversations, and on May 19 Gamelin concluded a military convention embracing Danzig. Gamelin, according to Bonnet, was taken in by the Polish story that a political agreement had already been signed—a version much removed from Gamelin's story, which puts the blame on Bonnet. At all events, the Poles, instead of being told that France could do nothing for them except strive for Russian aid, secured a French promise to launch a major offensive on the fifteenth day of mobilization. Thus, when the crisis arrived in August 1939, France had a military convention with Poland which vitiated her diplomacy and still lacked the military convention with the Soviet Union without which she could do nothing.

Bonnet claims always to have expected the crisis to arrive in August 1939. For him it remained a crisis of diplomacy; he aimed to stop Hitler by the show of a "peace front" in eastern Europe, and for this he had to reconcile two conflicting wills—the Soviet demand for military collaboration with Poland before war started and the Polish determination to accept Soviet aid only after the war had begun. On July 15, Noël, French Ambassador in Warsaw, reported: "M. Beck gave me to understand that the day war broke out Poland, the preservation of which the U.S.S.R. desires in its own interest, would be better placed than anyone else to obtain

from Moscow collaboration in a common action." Thus
French diplomacy had to sail as near the wind as possible—
to postpone the question of Soviet-Polish co-operation to a
moment which should still seem like peace to the Russians
but like war to the Poles.

The question was exploded by Voroshilov on August 14.
Bonnet launched his diplomatic offensive against the Poles
on August 16. He placed on Poland "the responsibility for
a failure of the military conversations with Moscow and for
all the consequences which would follow." And again, on
August 19, when the Poles repeated their refusal: "The
Polish Government must measure the full extent of its responsi-
bilities if its attitude should lead to the breaking off of negotiations with the U.S.S.R." The tone of this is not far removed
from the message of September 21, 1938, in which M. Bonnet
had declared French inability to help the Czechs. A concession
was finally extracted from Beck. On August 23 he told Noël
that the French could use the following language to the
Russians: "We have acquired the certainty that in the event
of common action against a German aggression collaboration
between Poland and the U.S.S.R., in technical conditions to
be determined, is not excluded (or: is possible)." No wonder
Molotov on August 25 "put all the responsibility on the
Government of Warsaw. A great country like the U.S.S.R.
could not, he said, go so far as to beg Poland to accept a
Russian assistance which she did not wish at any price."
In any case the Polish reply was fraudulent: it was given only
after the news of Ribbentrop's visit to Moscow was already
known and when therefore all chance of Soviet collaboration
had been lost. But then the Soviet demand was fraudulent
also, for the decision to receive Ribbentrop on August 23 was
communicated to the Germans on August 21, before
Voroshilov heard from the French of their failure to extract
any concessions from the Poles. In fact, as is usual in diplomacy,
all sides behaved in a discreditable fashion and put themselves
almost equally in the wrong.

The great manœuvre had failed. Thereafter Bonnet's
aim was to find an escape from the approaching war. After
all, he suggests, the Russians had insisted that they could not

fight Germany without a common frontier; the German conquest of Poland would provide one, and the Franco-Soviet pact could then be revived. On August 23 Bonnet asked Daladier to call the Committee of National Defence (actually the meeting was a less formal "Council of War") and there hinted, not obscurely, at this line: "Must we apply blindly our alliance with Poland? Would it be better, on the contrary, to push Warsaw into a compromise? We could thus gain time to perfect our material, to increase our military power, to improve our diplomatic situation in a manner to resist Germany more effectively in case she should turn against France later." Gamelin refused to play Bonnet's game: he would not confess France's military weakness and insisted on the value of the Polish alliance. Thus Bonnet successfully loaded on to Gamelin the decision in favour of war—as Gamelin implicitly admits by his later unconvincing attempts to question the validity of the record of the council meeting. In fact Bonnet could blame the generals for the failure of his diplomacy, as later the generals blamed the politicians for their military defeat.

Bonnet's last card was the attempted mediation of Mussolini. This, too, had to be delayed to the last minute; for the Poles, it was supposed, could be coerced into surrendering Danzig only at the very moment of the explosion of war. Bonnet continued to advocate accepting Mussolini's offer even after the German attack on Poland on September 1. Hence his anxiety to postpone the ultimatum to Germany until noon on Sunday, September 3. The British Government insisted on the preceding midnight, hostilities to begin at 6 a.m.; finally they compromised so far as to deliver the ultimatum at 9 a.m. (one hour before the meeting of Parliament), hostilities to begin at 11 a.m. At 5 a.m. on Sunday morning Bonnet heard of Ciano's final "Impossible!" to a further approach through De Monzie. Committed now to war, he became, by a last absurdity, the advocate of advancing the French time-table in order to keep up diplomatic appearances with the British.

The French ultimatum, presented at noon on Sunday, was to expire only at 5 a.m. the following morning: the

General Staff insisted on this delay. Complaints followed from London. At 11.30 on Sunday morning Daladier agreed to advance the opening of hostilities to 5 p.m. that afternoon. At 11.45 a.m. Bonnet telephoned to Coulondre, the Ambassador in Berlin, who was already leaving for the German Foreign Office, and informed him of the change. Coulondre had no doubt experienced Bonnet's telephone messages before. "With much presence of mind he asked that such news should be confirmed to him by one or two of my collaborators whose voice he would also recognize. I passed the telephone successively to M. Léger and to M. Bressy, who were by me." Bonnet spent the last few hours of peace drafting a Note for Warsaw which repudiated the Polish charges of delay and complained that Beck had failed to visit him in January: "Whatever the capital mistakes of the Polish Government have been in the past, history will record that no breach of honour or of the pledged word can be levelled against the French Government." On September 4 Bonnet signed the protocol to the Franco-Polish alliance which he had refused in May; this brought the military convention of May 19 automatically into operation and Bonnet was given a last chance to score off Gamelin, who failed to carry it out. On September 15 Bonnet left the Foreign Office. He received the following letter from Lord Halifax (retranslated from the French):

> When I received the news that you were leaving your crushing duties at the Quai d'Orsay I wished to write to you at once in order to say how much I have appreciated our collaboration and the friendly, personal relations which have sprung from it.
> We have together passed through the most difficult and the most depressing times that a Minister of Foreign Affairs has had to face: they have left us many bitter memories. But it is a great comfort for us to recall the loyal collaboration of our two Governments in mutual confidence and to have the conviction that it was impossible to follow any other policy.

The testimonial was somewhat flattering.

IV

GENERAL GAMELIN: OR HOW TO LOSE

GAMELIN, a generalissimo now forgotten, began his memoirs, it is said, on May 19, 1940, the day of his dismissal.[1] Even after the events of 1940 it was possible to discuss his military gifts; after his book, controversy is ended. There are limits to absurdity even in a soldier. Gamelin's wisest course would have been to remain silent, or at the very least to insert the events of 1940 in the general course of his memoirs, presenting his failure as the inevitable result of the failures of the preceding twenty years. Instead he repeats the mistake of the advance into Belgium: recognizing his weak points, he seeks to hide them by an impetuous advance —perhaps the enemy (in this case posterity), seeing him charge, will be taken in and will imagine him stronger than he is. His heaviest arm, used therefore in the first chapter, is an order to counter-attack, which he claims to have given at the moment of his dismissal on May 19—an order which, judged by its timid phrases and the circumstances of the moment, it is difficult to take seriously. His most vulnerable spot, tackled therefore in Chapter II, is the declaration which he is alleged to have made on August 23, 1939: "The army is ready." By this, it seems, he meant only: "The army is ready for the order for mobilization and concentration." Later he admits that even this was not true. As to the advance into Belgium, he falls back on political arguments: "Could France and England abandon Belgium, which they had always guaranteed? This would admit their helplessness." In any case, he adds, it was only by advancing into Belgium that a decisive battle could be provoked. This he certainly obtained.

The bulk of his first volume is devoted to proving that the French armies of 1940 were well equipped; this only serves

[1] *Servir.* I. Les Armées françaises de 1940. II. Le Prologue du drame. III. La Guerre. By General Gamelin.

to underline Gamelin's failure. He could plead, it is true, that his failure was not unique: the Russians made disastrous blunders in the summer of 1941 and the Anglo-American armies were surprised in the Ardennes as late as 1944. Their commanders learnt from their mistakes; Gamelin did not. He still talks in terms of a continuous line of defence and knows no method of resisting an attack other than fighting "without retreat," a sure recipe for disaster.

The second volume, which runs from his appointment as second-in-command to Weygand in 1930 until the outbreak of war in 1939, is of more value to the historian. Gamelin owed his position to his gifts as a conciliator. He was loyal to the civilian Ministers, never intrigued against them, always tried to make their paths easy. As he complacently remarks on more than one occasion, his motto was "Servir." The motto was hardly the most suitable for the commander-in-chief of a great army, but it made him a good politician and diplomatist. Naturally he never obtained all the credits that he asked; but his book contains no evidence that he would have known how to use them, even if he had obtained them. Since French economic resources were limited, how could they be best employed? Gamelin never envisaged this question; he followed the military principles of an earlier age, when men and not machines decided the lot of war. Besides, even if French resources were used more wisely, could France still hope to undertake a great offensive war? If not, should not her international policy be changed from top to bottom? The politicians asked Gamelin the first question; neither they nor he dared ask the second.

Faced with the question of an offensive war, Gamelin was placed in an inescapable dilemma. If he admitted that the French armies could not invade Germany, the politicians would demand what had happened to their money and perhaps refuse further supplies. Gamelin had therefore to answer that the French army could perform its task, if only a little more money was spent on it. But he had to cover himself against the time when the additional money had been spent and the question was asked again. He therefore always added: the French army could act only if France was supported by her allies. Thus France built up a system of alliances in eastern Europe which rested on the assumption that France could attack Germany without British assistance; yet Gamelin would promise an offensive only if England was in alliance with France and if her eastern allies would co-operate against Germany. In short, to make the offensive possible, Gamelin insisted on alliances which would make it unnecessary. But as his sole diplomatic argument was the offensive capacity of the French armies, this landed Gamelin in new contradictions.

His dilemma was clearly shown when the Germans reoccupied the Rhineland on March 7, 1936. German rearmament had only begun; France had been able to maintain her army without restrictions. French territory was fortified; the Rhineland was open. Yet the only assurance that Gamelin could give was that French soil would not be invaded; he could take a "pledge" of German territory only on condition of complete mobilization, and he could expel the German forces from the Rhineland only after a long war, in which Belgian and British support would be necessary. Thus, once again, when the politicians asked a military question, Gamelin returned a diplomatist's answer.

So, too, during the Spanish civil war and the crisis of Munich, Gamelin, on paper, was always in favour of resistance; but he always attached conditions—a total war-effort in France and effective British assistance—which the politicians were unable to fulfil. The French army can take the offensive against Germany (therefore the money spent on it has not been wasted); it cannot finish off the job alone (therefore more money must be spent on it and allies must be found). Still, Gamelin regarded war in 1938 as practical and even believed that the Czechs could hold out in Moravia; perhaps he gave his judgment the more confidently because he knew all along that the politicians had decided against war, and he was glad to embarrass them. Gamelin had a much poorer opinion of the Poles than of the Czechs, and disapproved of the guarantee given to Poland in March 1939; it should have been conditional, he says, on the Poles agreeing to the passage of a Russian army across their territory. Yet on May 18, 1939, Gamelin signed a military convention with the

Poles, by which he promised that "France would launch an offensive action with the bulk (*les gros*) of her forces on the fifteenth day after the first day of French mobilization." His defence of this discreditable transaction is remarkable. It was not, he says, a promise to use the bulk (*le gros*) of the French army against Germany, but only to use the forces (*les gros*) mobilized in the front line. Besides, he says, the military convention was signed by mistake and was never valid. It was meant to be the sequel to a political agreement with the Poles, defining more closely the obligations of the Franco-Polish alliance. Once the military convention was drafted the Poles were satisfied. Bonnet, French Foreign Minister, was also satisfied; for the Poles were now committed to launching an offensive if Germany attacked France, yet he could always plead that France was not committed without the political agreement. Therefore the political agreement was dropped. Even this argument does not excuse Gamelin. The political agreement was, in fact, signed on September 1, 1939, after the outbreak of war; and the impossible obligation of May 18 then came into operation. These are specious excuses. In 1939 the traditional policy of France had collapsed and France behaved like the chicken which continues to run round the farmyard after its head has been cut off.

With his third volume Gamelin at last arrives at the period of the war. Even now he is most concerned to show the correctness of his behaviour. He was never guilty of an intrigue, of a harsh word, of an act of betrayal; alas, he was also never guilty of a victory. Gamelin's personal contribution to the war was "the offensive for Poland." The offensive satisfied Gamelin's honour; it did not help the Poles. It was launched on condition that *it* involved no risk to the French; it therefore involved no risk also to the Germans. Gamelin called off this timorous offensive even before the collapse of Poland and boasts of the skilful withdrawal without casualties—as though the Germans minded whether the French withdrew or not. Gamelin dared not stay in the Saar even when the German armies were still in Poland; yet the following May he flung his armies into Belgium when all the German armies were in the west.

When Poland was conquered, the "phoney" war began.
"What next?" was the baffling question facing the Allies in
the winter of 1939–40, discussed again and again without
result. The Allies hoped that Hitler would make his first
move in the Balkans; this, they calculated, would give them
"a hundred divisions" (without equipment and untrained for
modern war!). Since Hitler failed to "solve" their problem
for them, the Allies looked north and south—to the iron
mines of Sweden and the oil wells of Baku. Darlan wished
to bomb Baku and to send submarines into the Black Sea.
When it was pointed out that this would need Turkish permission and would involve war with Russia, he replied that these
were problems which the politicians must solve. But, Gamelin
adds, in any case there were no aeroplanes in the Middle East
capable of bombing Baku; Darlan was proposing an impossible scheme merely for the pleasure of blaming the
politicians. Gamelin himself favoured an expedition to Narvik
in order to "draw out" the Germans. The Allies hoped that if
they threatened the Germans at points of less importance,
the Germans would overlook the fact that they could threaten
the Allies at the point of decisive importance—on the western
front.

Yet, far from diverting the Germans, the Allies could not
even take precautions against them. The Belgian problem
baffled both soldiers and politicians. The Allies knew that they
could not defend Belgium effectively unless they entered
before the Germans; yet they dared not force an entry by
threatening to leave Belgium to her fate. Fearful of German
preponderance, they exaggerated the value of swelling their
forces with the Belgian divisions, and for the sake of the Belgian
army lost their own. Besides, as Gamelin points out, the frontier
between Belgium and France was unfortified, so that once the
Germans had conquered Belgium they could invade France
at their leisure. The French army, equipped for defensive
warfare, had no line of defence on which to meet a German
attack. Gamelin's "solution" was to prophesy a war of movement. This was more intelligent than those who relied confidently on a continuous defence; only his intelligence led to
no useful conclusion. Gamelin would have made a more

effective excuse if he had confessed the mistake that he shared with everyone else—with every French general, with the British, with the Russians, and with every German except Hitler: though he expected that the Germans might over-run Belgium and perhaps part of northern France, he also expected that they would be stopped somewhere. The Belgian campaign had to be faced, like having a tooth out; after it the front would be stabilized, and the Allies could begin to build up their strength for a counter-offensive in 1941 and 1942. Gamelin shared, too, the universal error that the only answer to the Blitzkrieg was to meet it head on. Later, the British in North Africa and then the Russians stumbled on the true answer much against their will: the only solution was to run very far and very fast.

Gamelin has little to say about the decisive days between May 10 and May 19, the only days of his life which will give him a place in the history books—or at least a footnote. May 10 ended the period of political manœuvre, began the conflict of real forces; and there was no place for Gamelin, the political soldier. His book tails off as though he had become a ghost, all life evaporating from him as the guns began to fire. Even now Gamelin is mainly concerned to prove his correct behaviour: he left General Georges freedom of action and so responsibility before posterity. It would have been better to be less correct and more successful; rudeness to General Georges could have been overlooked if it had also defeated the Germans. Can one imagine Foch or Joffre, Gamelin's master, standing by in philosophical detachment while a subordinate general led the French armies to hopeless defeat? Gamelin cannot escape the position of having been in supreme command of the army which suffered the greatest disaster in history since the battle of Jena. Joffre said of the battle of the Marne: "I do not know if I won it, but I know who would have been responsible if it had been lost."

V

THE END OF THE THIRD REPUBLIC

PAUL REYNAUD was the last Prime Minister of the Third Republic. His evidence on the defeat of France might be expected to have great historical value. Unfortunately in his two bulky volumes[1] evidence is overlaid with advocacy. His object is not to record but to prove: to prove that on every issue of financial, military and foreign policy between the wars he was right and others—especially Petain, who betrayed and supplanted him—wrong. Reynaud wages against his critics a more successful war than he waged against the Germans. Even the title of his book is provocative; never explained or justified, it remains an isolated stroke of cleverness. When old controversies are constantly raked over, an individual or a nation is living in the past instead of facing the present. No doubt Reynaud is usually right in his criticisms. Still, instead of showing why everyone else failed, it would have been more useful to show why he himself did not succeed. It is not enough for a politician to have the correct views: he must secure some backing and be able to put them into operation. Clémenceau, too, had long periods of unpopularity; but in the crisis he struck a note which reverberated in the hearts of millions of Frenchmen. Reynaud remained the man of the unanswerable argument and the telling phrase; this was the tragedy of his career.

Reynaud had certainly a feeling for the dramatic moment. He understood that war demands action rather than philosophical musings. He imposed the expedition to Narvik on Gamelin; and Gamelin acquiesced in the hope that it would distract Darlan from Baku and the Germans from the western front. Reynaud hoped to strike a decisive blow at Narvik; he achieved only a striking phrase. The weaker party cannot strike a decisive blow: he can only bring it on himself. Reynaud would, no doubt, have made a more forceful general

---

[1] *La France a Sauvé l'Europe.* By Paul Reynaud. Two volumes.

than Gamelin, just as Gamelin would have made a more conciliatory premier than Reynaud. Both lacked any grasp of the realities of power. Gamelin could describe the weakness of the French army on paper; he could not draw any useful conclusion. Reynaud recognized the French need for political leadership; he could not supply it. He had no party in the Chamber, no following in the country and little experience of responsible government. He had no contact with the French people and served French "honour" rather than any political community. His brilliant wireless talks leave the impression of being delivered to a microphone that is not "live." He himself complains that he was never in control of his Cabinet; and he became Minister of War only on May 18. Clémenceau would not have tolerated such a position.

Reynaud's first attempt to infuse more energy into affairs was against Gamelin. When Daladier defended Gamelin on May 9 Reynaud intended to resign and to reconstruct his Ministry the following day. The German invasion of Belgium interrupted this manœuvre. On May 18 he tried again. He got rid of Gamelin and shifted Daladier from the Ministry of War. To raise French morale he called in the two "heroes" of the first German war, Petain and Weygand. This was his supreme blunder. He had been, he pleads, too busy advocating the devaluation of the franc to study military affairs before the war. But is it not the business of a saviour of his country to understand military affairs and to know in advance which men to choose? Reynaud had been in close touch with de Gaulle and had learnt from him the fundamental weakness of the French military system. Ignorance cannot be his excuse. His real excuse he does not make: he felt his divorce from the French masses and needed to be reinforced by two great names.

Reynaud was now the prisoner of his own cleverness. Having called in the two "heroes," he dared not turn them out again. Instead he planned to make them harmless. This was the object of his reconstruction of the Cabinet on June 5, designed to put Petain safely in the minority. A plausible defence. Still, if he wished to strengthen the party of resistance, why get rid of Daladier, a failure, perhaps, as an administrator, but a reliable patriot? With Daladier gone, Reynaud had to rely on Chautemps as the representative Radical, and this reliance was his undoing. From Chautemps came the insidious suggestion to ask the Germans their armistice terms merely to demonstrate that these would be unacceptable. Reynaud could answer only by a counter-manœuvre: to ask the British Government to release France from her pledge not to negotiate a separate armistice, in the expectation that the British would refuse. He expected to find in Churchill the ruthlessness and inspiration which he could not find in himself. Reynaud was deserted by his Cabinet and resigned. Even then he manœuvred with a false judgment of personalities. He said bitterly: "If you want to follow this policy, invite Marshal Petain," expecting, even on June 16, that Petain would act with more patriotism than a civilian.

Still, in the confusion of defeat, no man could have acted wisely. Reynaud, with his intellectual honesty, admits the real blunder of 1940. From the moment of the German breakthrough at Sedan Generals Georges and Gamelin ought to have recognized the inescapable alternative—armistice or withdrawal to North Africa—and Weygand ought to have done the same when he succeeded Gamelin. The generals failed. Reynaud ought then to have taken the responsibility on himself and, from May 16 onwards, subordinated everything to preparing the continuation of the war in North Africa. Instead, he dreamt of a "moral" recovery and placed his faith in generals who had prepared the disaster.

His deepest mistake he does not admit, for it cannot be grasped by his detached intellect. Every country has its patterns of political behaviour. France could not be saved by political manœuvres or by calling on exhausted reputations of the first German war. The French answer to crisis was Jacobinism—the course of revolutionary terror; this was the course that Clémenceau took in 1917. A French Prime Minister who made a clean sweep of the generals and who imprisoned or executed the advocates of surrender might not have stopped the German advance; but he would have saved France for the future. On May 3, 1940, de Gaulle wrote to Reynaud: "In France the great man of this war will be Carnot or no one." Reynaud was not Carnot.

VI

DR. SCHACHT'S DEFENCE

A BALANCING of accounts is often a weapon of defence;
and Dr. Schacht's settlement with Hitler is also a defence
of his own action. His book[1] has been deservedly a best-seller
in Germany; a defence which has carried its author unscathed
through the Nuremberg tribunal and subsequent German
inquiries is not to be despised. It is by far the most revealing
analysis which has come out of post-war Germany and,
moreover, the only work by one who held high office under
Hitler. Though a defence, it is not an apology. Self-confident,
supremely clever, detached, Dr. Schacht was never moved by
enthusiasm for Hitler, and has remained equally unaffected
by the general repudiation of him. He explains in measured
terms why he accepted office under Hitler, and in equally
measured terms why he left office and attempted to organize
Hitler's overthrow. As becomes a good banker, Dr. Schacht
is sparing of everything, even of facts: there are no revelations and even few concrete statements, but these few are used
with decisive effect.

The rise of the Nazis, Dr. Schacht argues, was due to the
failure of the democratic parties: Hitler offered "the brutality
of action." If Schacht is accused of helping Hitler to power,
then the 14,000,000 Germans who voted for Hitler must be
accused also. In 1933 the Nazis had 40 per cent. of the votes,
"more than any party had had since the creation of the
Reichstag"; and the only alternative to Hitler was a military
dictatorship. "True to my democratic convictions, I was
against a military dictatorship and in favour of a Cabinet of
National Socialists." Schacht, like many others, hoped that
Hitler would be tamed by constitutional power. Instead,
Schacht complains, the Reichstag passed the Enabling Act
which gave Hitler's dictatorship legal sanction, and the

[1] *Abrechnung mit Hitler.* By Dr. Hjalmar Schacht.

non-Nazi Ministers made no attempt to maintain themselves.
The Social Democrats voted for Hitler's declaration of foreign
policy, and the Socialist ex-Ministers continued to draw their
pensions. Similarly, the Army did nothing to protest against
the murder of Schleicher or the dismissal of Fritsch.

One Minister tried to keep Hitler within bounds—
protected the Jews, resisted Nazi interference in his department, and rejected Hitler's wild economic schemes. This
was Dr. Schacht, Minister of Economics: "I undertook the
task before which the democratic leaders had taken flight."
In 1937 Schacht lost his battle with Goering and resigned
his Ministry, in spite of Hitler's pleading. Thereafter he
organized resistance as president of the Reichsbank; and
early in 1939, when Hitler took to financing rearmament by
open inflation, Schacht submitted a protest signed by all the
directors of the Bank. This was the only open opposition to
Hitler ever made by any German institution or organization;
and Schacht is perhaps right in claiming that if only others
had followed the example of the Bank Hitler would not have
found it so easy to have things all his own way. As it was,
Schacht achieved only a personal satisfaction. Hitler reproached
him for having criticized the pogrom of November 1938,
in front of his subordinates. Schacht replied: 'If I had known
that you approved of these events I should have kept silent."
Hitler exploded: "I am too excited to discuss any more with
you," and Schacht answered quietly: "I can come again
when you are calmer." It was a virtuoso scene and, given
Schacht's self-possession in equally difficult circumstances,
probably a true one.

From this moment Schacht stood aside from the fortunes
of the Nazi Reich, though he could not divest himself of his
Ministerial title. This title meant nothing: the Reich Cabinet,
he says, never met after 1937 (in another passage he says
that it met for the last time in 1938 to receive in silence the
news of the dismissal of Fritsch). Moreover, Schacht claims
to have been associated with Witzleben in the project for
overthrowing Hitler in 1938 during the Munich crisis. He
bases this claim on the evidence of Gisevius and is careful
not to add any of his own: indeed, he was too discreet to

create any evidence. He speaks contemptuously of the later efforts at "resistance." When one conspirator showed him a manifesto beginning "Hitler is dead," he remarked that the manifesto could wait until the fact was true. He points out, too, that there was no effective conspiracy on July 20, 1944: it was an isolated act by Stauffenberg, and the "conspirators," though numbering Field-Marshals and ex-Ministers, were at a loss what action to take.

His contempt is not reserved for his fellow-countrymen. As he says, foreigners succumbed just as weakly to the Hitler terror, though they had less excuse for doing so. In foreign policy Schacht differed from Hitler in method, not in aim. Like any Nazi ranter, he blames all Germany's troubles on the Treaty of Versailles—as though unemployment were a complaint peculiar to Germany—and he repeats the stale fiction that all would have been well if Germany had been excused reparations and granted equality of armaments.

Even stranger, he treats the return of the colonies as the solution of Germany's economic problems, and claims that this would have distracted Hitler's attention from south-eastern Europe. Yet it was here that planned foreign trade, which was the essence of "Schachtism," won its great victories. Moreover, he proposes to solve Germany's present difficulties by organizing the whole of European economic life and eliminating all competition in international trade. As he slyly remarks, the devices which he invented fifteen years ago are now the commonplace of every democratic Government; and he might have added that "Schachtism," with the exploitation of the colonies thrown in, exhausts the Socialism of some of the extreme left-wingers of the British Labour party. Schacht's proposals would give Germany by peaceful means the domination of Europe which Hitler failed to win by violence. This is the decisive argument against them. Schacht has never understood that the peoples of Europe do not wish to be controlled by Germany, even if this control is established peacefully and according to accepted bankers' rules.

Schacht always omitted feeling and emotion from his political calculation; hence his failure. Dr. Schacht is a very clever man and, in his way, a civilized man, faithful to his banker's code of ethics, even a good member of the Confessional Church. Yet he was helpless against Hitler. It was the story of Talleyrand and Napoleon over again: the clever, sensible man of ideas could achieve nothing against the genius of action. Hitler, like Napoleon, understood that politics are a matter of power and of emotion, not of calculation; and he saw, too, that conquest was the only method by which German domination of Europe could be established. Much against Schacht's will the man against whom the account is drawn dominates Schacht's book. Hitler was "without a home, without a family, without friends, without women, without a church, without tradition." For this very reason he incorporated Germany; he was a genius—a genius of will, of resourcefulness, of organization. He was a titanic demon. Against such, cleverness is not enough.

VII

JACKAL DIPLOMACY

THOUGH Ciano spent a frivolous and worthless life he put the world in his debt by the diaries and papers which he left. The Diary for 1939 to 1942 was a splendid source of information on recent history. The papers of the present volume[1] were assembled by Ciano as a supplement to the Diary; they were sometimes included and very often referred to in it. These papers are mainly Ciano's own notes of conversations with foreign diplomatists and statesmen, with summaries of Mussolini's similar conversations thrown in. They are more formal and less entertaining than the Diary, without light relief or personal anecdotes; on the other hand they cover the whole period from 1936 to 1942, when Ciano was Foreign Minister, and are therefore particularly valuable for the pre-war period omitted in the Diary, as so far published here.

The volume opens in the days of Italy's greatness, Abyssinia conquered, the League of Nations humiliated and the League Powers apologetically removing sanctions. Austria and Hungary were under Italian protection; and even Germany behaved as a junior partner. In October 1936 Hitler welcomed Italian co-operation against England: "We must go over to the attack. And the tactical field on which we must execute the manœuvre is that of anti-Bolshevism." In January 1937 Goering was warned that Germany must leave Austria alone. At this meeting Goering and Mussolini agreed "to push matters to the limit" in Spain; the limit was the risk of a general war. In other words, non-intervention, far from preventing a general war (as was claimed at the time), encouraged aggressors hitherto cautious and helped to cause general war. In the course of 1937 Germany gradually assumed the dominating role. In November 1937 Mussolini

---

[1] *Ciano's Diplomatic Papers.* Edited by Malcolm Muggeridge.

virtually renounced Austria to Ribbentrop: "He is tired of mounting guard over Austrian independence, especially if the Austrians no longer want their independence." The Austrian crisis of February 1938 produced a twinge of alarm; and Grandi was instructed to warn the British Government that, after the Anschluss, Italy must pass completely into the German orbit.

Before this instruction reached Grandi, Chamberlain made his first independent sally into foreign policy. He seems to have thought that if he gave way to Italy on every question from Spain to Abyssinia, Italy in return would oppose the Anschluss. Grandi was summoned to a meeting with Chamberlain and Mr. Eden; and the conflict between them was fought out in his presence. Chamberlain asked whether there was a secret agreement between Germany and Italy by which Italy renounced Austria in exchange for German backing in the Mediterranean. Grandi was able truthfully to deny this (the Pact of Steel was still in the future); and Chamberlain then took him point by point through the objections which Mr. Eden had made. In Grandi's words:

> The questions and queries addressed to me by Chamberlain were all, without exception, intentionally put with the aim of producing replies which would have the effect of contradicting and overthrowing the bases of argument on which Eden had evidently previously constructed, or by which he had attempted to justify, his miserable anti-Italian and anti-Fascist policy in opposition to Chamberlain and before his colleagues in the Cabinet.

To complete the effect, Chamberlain conveyed a private message through a man (named in the Italian edition) that "he sent me cordial greetings and appreciated my statements, which had been very useful to him." No more discreditable transaction has ever been recorded of a British Prime Minister; no wonder Grandi wrote patronizingly of Chamberlain's "cobbler forefathers in Birmingham." Though Mr. Eden resigned, his expectations were justified. Mussolini accepted all the concessions and did nothing in exchange. Yet even in January 1939, during the Rome visit, "neither Chamberlain nor Halifax have ever doubted the good faith of the Duce," and Chamberlain asked Mussolini's advice how to keep Hitler within bounds.

By then Italy had ceased to be able to follow an independent course. The last Italian score over Germany had been the backing of Hungarian claims against post-Munich Czechoslovakia in November 1938; according to Ciano, arbitration by Germany and Italy, though a breach of the Munich agreement, was regarded by London "not only without prejudice but with satisfaction"—the men of Munich kept their word only when it injured Czechoslovakia. In February 1939 Ciano attempted to create an Italo-Yugoslav barrier against Germany; this attempt collapsed with the fall of Stoyadinović in March. In May, Ciano met Ribbentrop with the hope of restraining German action against Poland; instead, he was abruptly ordered by Mussolini to conclude a military alliance, the Pact of Steel. At this meeting Ribbentrop gave the first hint that Germany hoped to "continue and increase the *detente* which has arisen between the Axis and the Soviet Union." Ciano next met Ribbentrop at Salzburg on August 11. Ribbentrop, and later Hitler, told him that war with Poland had been irrevocably fixed for the end of August. Hitler said: "France and England will certainly make extremely theatrical anti-German gestures but will not go to war." He also said: "In the last few days there has been a Russian request for the dispatch of a German Plenipotentiary to Moscow."

Ciano recorded every phase of the Nazi-Soviet friendship. In October 1939 Ribbentrop was "more and more infatuated with Russia"; "among the members of the Politburo and of the Comintern he felt himself as comfortable as amongst the old guard of Nazism or the old squadristi . . . the Comintern no longer exists and Stalin has become in effect the champion of Russian Nationalism." A year later, in October 1940, Hitler said: "The distrust on my side towards Stalin is matched by Stalin's distrust towards me." Russian "dynamism" was to be directed towards Persia and Afghanistan. The Russians, however, refused this plausible offer and began to encroach in the Balkans and the Straits; they were once more "that faithless country," and war against Russia was only a matter of time, though the Italians were warned of this only on June 15, 1941. Italy was more directly involved in the attempts to bring Spain into the war in autumn 1940 and early in 1941. Franco was profuse in good wishes: "The Spanish, too, believe firmly in the victory of the Axis." He always found an excuse against action: he made demands for wheat and oil, pleaded the defencelessness of the Canaries, insisted on large-scale military assistance. Above all, he demanded Oran and all Morocco, terms which would have estranged Vichy France and even Italy. After the meeting at Hendaye, "rather than go through it again the Fuehrer would prefer to have three or four teeth taken out." Mussolini tried in February 1941, with equal lack of success. Ciano met Suñer for the last time in Berlin in November 1941 and wrote in alarm: "He says things with a brutality that makes one jump in one's chair. When leaving he commented: 'No doubt this man is very formidable because of his enormous military power. However, I don't find him interesting.'" The time had long passed when Ciano, or even Mussolini, could speak of Hitler with such frankness.

VIII

THE SUPERMEN: HITLER AND MUSSOLINI

A GREAT idea seldom gets a free run. The scientist in his laboratory can concentrate on a single line of research and work it to fruition—or to death. In the world of real life experiments are always being interrupted or broken off half-way. Thus, the policy of treating the Germans resolutely was broken off by the French in 1923 just when it was succeeding: and the policy of co-operating with the Russians was broken off in 1945 before the rewards (and difficulties) of this policy became plain. The great question of the future is whether mankind will turn against the scientists before they succeed in blowing up the planet—certainly an experiment of great interest. One idea has had a real run for its money—tried out without restriction and carried to its extreme. This is the idea of the Hero or Superman, the political saviour for whom many Europeans have been craving ever since the time of Napoleon. The myth was launched by Napoleon himself and took his own nephew prisoner; Carlyle preached it with religious frenzy; Wagner dressed it up in musical form for the Germans; and in the early twentieth century practically every writer offered some form of anti-democratic, superman doctrine.

Twenty years later the superman arrived—or rather two supermen arrived, Mussolini and Hitler, Napoleons of the twentieth century, the heroes of our time. Both were pure-hero types, without any of the adventitious aids of their predecessors. Frederick the Great inherited his crown; Napoleon had a background of military success; Cromwell and Lenin rested on a compact revolutionary class. Hitler and Mussolini made themselves. Except as heroes, they were nobodies. Before they attained power, they had achieved nothing; and the supposed class-basis of their rule (Fascism is the last stage of Capitalism) was arrant nonsense. Their real supporters were men as classless as themselves, not great capitalists or even the petty *bourgeoisie*. General Beck said of Hitler: "this man has no country," and one could add—no class, no past, no family. Mussolini had a family and even a mistress: this did not prevent his ordering the execution of his son-in-law. Certainly he sometimes repeated "proletarian" echoes of his past, as Hitler lived on the Greater German rhetoric that he had picked up in Vienna. These were merely incantations, phrases to produce the popular roar; not genuine beliefs, still less the motives of their action. These heroes believed only in themselves. Like all men in public life, they craved for power. The exceptional thing in them was the addition of intense personal vanity: they wished both to stand in the limelight and to control the switchboard, to be actor, producer and playwright. In short, they wished to be God; and mankind having lost its faith in God, acquiesced in their wish.

Heroes are not of mortal clay; that we know of all supermen from Siegfried to Jack Tanner. We cannot expect them to act according to normal standards or even to notice the human beings around them. But how do they get on with each other? This is the fascinating topic of Miss Wiskemann's book[1]: the relations of the two supermen. According to all authorities, heroes recognize each other instinctively: they keep faith with each other, though they betray all the world besides. Miss Wiskemann attributes to Hitler and Mussolini a common intellectual ancestry: she puts all the blame on Nietzsche. This seems to me too narrow a basis: there is little to it except that Hitler once fell into a trance before the bust of the master. It leaves out of account the long hero-tradition in modern Europe. Mussolini summed up the Latin line of that tradition from Bonaparte to Georges Sorel; Hitler sprang directly from Carlyle and Wagner. More deeply (and this is the sense in the hero-idea) each in his way expressed the "genius" of his people—a parody, no doubt, as summaries always are, but no more a parody than Churchill, say, is of the British people. One can safely adapt for both Hitler and Mussolini Gardiner's phrase about Cromwell: "the greatest,

[1] *The Rome-Berlin Axis*. By Elizabeth Wiskemann.

because the most typical Englishman of all time." Of course both men were lunatics, as Miss Wiskemann firmly establishes of Hitler, though doubtfully of Mussolini (such is her soft-heartedness for all Italians). The point is not of moment. All men are mad who devote themselves to the pursuit of power when they could be fishing, painting pictures, or simply sitting in the sun. If men were sane, there would be no history. Though lunatics do not follow the rules of sane behaviour, they have rules of their own. The task of the historian is to discover these rules. No man acts out of character; and, as Machiavelli said, a man has only one character, as he has only one face. Hitler's rules and character ran true to a form that is easily mapped; Mussolini's behaviour was more complicated and therefore Miss Wiskemann inclines to believe him sane —or suffering from a duodenal ulcer, which comes to the same thing. There is a more profound explanation: even the hero cannot escape reality, even he remains rooted in the ground from which he has sprung.

Miss Wiskemann disapproves of such high subjects as Hitler and Mussolini being treated by "witty Oxford dons" (alas! this is not a reference to the present writer). Wit has its advantages: it puts the hero in his historic setting. The difference between Hitler and Mussolini was the difference between their two countries. In Miss Wiskemann's book Germany and Italy come in too little. They are treated as two sovereign States of comparable importance; there is no analysis of their historic background or (apart from a table of Italy's coal imports) of their economic strength. The coal statistics give the game away. Coal is the most important index of power. Italy has no coal; therefore she is dependent for her power on others, condemned to a jackal diplomacy—or to none at all. The hesitations and manœuvres of Mussolini were not, as Miss Wiskemann thinks, the results of doubt so much as a hero's resentment against the limitations of real life—truly, Mussolini was a hero of the suburbs. Vain and arrogant as he was, he yet had the sense to see that Italy could simulate greatness only by hunting with Hitler: he never shared the futile misjudgment of those western diplomats who thought that Italy could take the place of

Russia in an anti-Hitler coalition (a favourite idea of the
British foreign office), and he never accepted for a moment
the ambition of Italian diplomats, from Ciano downwards,
to play fast-and-loose with Germany and yet swagger among
the great. Hitler saw the dilemma just as clearly. He wrote
to Mussolini on March 6, 1940:

> The outcome of this war will also decide the future of Italy. If this future
> is considered in your country in terms of merely perpetuating the existence
> of a European state of modest pretensions, then I am wrong. But if this future
> is considered in terms of a guarantee of the existence of the Italian people
> from a historical, geopolitical and moral point of view, or according to the
> rights of your people, those who are fighting Germany to-day will be your
> enemies too.

Against this profound analysis, Miss Wiskemann concludes: "It was not mere rhetoric to say that one Italian alone
forced Italy into the war in June 1940." It is all very well to
like Italians better than Germans. Who doesn't? This does
not alter the fact that Germany was (and is) the only country
on the European continent of Great Power stature; and that
Italy could be carried to greatness only on Germany's back.
Miss Wiskemann writes as though the Axis was an aberration
of Mussolini's; in reality it came at the end of a tradition
which includes Charlemagne and Napoleon, Metternich and
Bismarck.

This, indeed, is the most curious thing about these
heroes. According to the prophets, they were to be men
without a past, beyond good and evil, and—what is more
important—beyond tradition and habit. Both Hitler and
Mussolini tried to follow the teachings of the prophetic
books. They invented their uniforms and their methods of
address—Duce and Fuehrer, titles never heard before. They
wrote each other interminable letters, which were meant to
be the correspondence of gods. Miss Wiskemann quotes a
description by Shirer of the signing of the Pact with Japan:
"Three loud knocks on the giant door are heard. There is a
tense hush in the great hall. The Japanese hold their breath.
The door swings slowly open and in strides Hitler." It is like a
scene from *The Great Dictator*, except that no one is allowed
to laugh. Yet as soon as it comes to practical affairs, these

heroes turn out to be creatures of history like anyone else. Hitler's ideas were the commonplace of pan-Germans in Vienna; Mussolini's policy is what one would expect from a countryman of Cavour and Crispi. Thus the history of the Axis is a story on two planes. On one level it expressed merely the personality of two lunatics; on the other it was a profoundly important chapter in the diplomacy of Germany and Italy, the two revolutionary nations of 1848. This contradiction baffled the two heroes themselves. As the only gods in Europe, they ought to have been on terms of peculiar confidence, faithfully united against all others. This was the impression they tried to give to the world and even to themselves: each believed in the other—Mussolini was hypnotized by Hitler, and Hitler was genuinely taken in by Mussolini. All the same, the pull of real life was too strong for them. Hitler despised Mussolini at the very moment of believing in him; Mussolini knew that Hitler was leading him to disaster, even though he followed him with conviction. Each tricked the other and intrigued against the other though each knew that this was a sin against the hero in himself. Thus Mussolini encouraged the Czechs to become Communists in the autumn of 1939 in order to make things difficult between Moscow and Berlin; he protected Polish refugees and even hoped that Yugoslavia would be a barrier against German expansion in the Balkans. Hitler kept German irredentism in Tyrol up his sleeve, cut down Italy's share of Yugoslavia after its conquest, rejected Italy's claims against France. As a final oddity, though both were liars without restraint or scruple, each swallowed the other's lies and then was genuinely hurt at having been deceived. Probably each was happiest in the last phase, securely divorced from reality, Mussolini rattling the bones of the Fascist Republic and dreaming of St. Helena, Hitler reading Carlyle and preparing a stupendous *Götterdämmerung*. Both ran true to form to the end. Hitler's last letter reproached Mussolini for having lost the war by invading Greece; Mussolini carried this letter in his pocket to show that he had been the first of the resisters. In these last acts each expressed national character as well as his own—the hard-luck story of the German, the smart intrigue of the Italian.

They were a very nasty and ridiculous pair. The worst part of the story is that millions of people believed in them and applauded their every action. No doubt men deserved what they got, when they went around crying for a hero, a human saviour, a superman, instead of making the best of their own virtues and defects. Perhaps the Axis will sicken humanity with heroes for a long time to come. But I doubt it. Despite Miss Wiskemann, despite witty Oxford dons, Hitler and Mussolini seem safe for Valhalla.

IX

THE SPRINGS OF SOVIET DIPLOMACY

SCHOLARS once combed the Scriptures for polemical texts; now the Powers fling at each other fragments from the German archives, a more long-winded and less elegant substitute. The Americans launched the campaign with "Nazi-Soviet Relations, 1939–1941" (even the title is polemical); the Russians have retaliated with documents on Munich. Since the Americans had no foreign policy before the war, it is impossible to discredit them (or the reverse); therefore, the Russian counter-blow, so far as it hits anyone (which is not much), misses them and lands on the British —a symbol of present international relations. We get the knocks intended for the Americans. When Bismarck started this type of appeal with French documents captured during the Franco-German war, there was perhaps a "world-opinion" affected by it; and the Germans were even more successful with the documents which they published between the wars. Hitler's success would hardly have been possible without the guilty conscience in England and America which the forty volumes of German documents did much to create.

This world opinion no longer exists, and each side publishes documents merely in order to bolster its own convictions. British opinion is not likely to be shaken by the discovery that when Chamberlain and Halifax negotiated with Hitler, they did so in the hope of reaching an agreement with him. The same charity is not extended to the Russians. The *Economist* headed its account of the Nazi-Soviet documents, "When Stalin toasted Hitler." What else was he expected to do? After all, Stalin has toasted other notorious anti-Bolsheviks. Even Professor Namier, previously reticent in his judgments on Soviet policy, after reading "Nazi-Soviet Relations," spoke of "Stalin's war-guilt." These condemnations

are based on the view that the Soviet effort at collaboration
with the Germans was sincere. Other commentators have
taken a smarter line and have accused the Soviet Government
of cheating the Germans. The moral is clear: since they cheated
in their deals with the Germans, they will cheat us, too, and
therefore, I suppose (though this is not said so openly), we
had better apply Hitler's remedy. Pseudo-historical specula-
tion by journalists is not really very profitable, except to the
writers; and the historical conclusions which can be drawn
from "Nazi-Soviet Relations, 1939–1941," are of a more
humdrum character.

Still, conclusions can be drawn. Since the Franco-Soviet
pact was stillborn, the Nazi-Soviet pact of August 23, 1939,
marked the first appearance of Russia as a European Great
Power since the revolution. Like traditional Russian foreign
policy (including the original Franco-Russian alliance), Soviet
policy in 1939 aimed to keep out of Europe, not to return to
it; or, more strictly, to keep Europe out of Russia. Between
August 1939 and June 1941 Soviet policy worked for a
cordon sanitaire in reverse. The Baltic States and the Western
(Polish) Ukraine were the first stage; Finland and Bulgaria
the second; the straits leading from the Baltic and Black
Seas a more remote third. These latter steps were represented
to the Germans as a defence against England, to the British
as a defence against Germany; in reality they were both—the
cordon sanitaire does not discriminate in the germ-carriers
that it bars. Soviet statesmen claim to be far-sighted; in fact,
their programme of 1939 was mostly improvised. Since 1917
they had only the experience of warding off dangers, never of
making demands. In 1939 they were courted by both sides
and brushed up the diplomacy of twenty years before; after
all, States, like individuals, can only start again where they
left off. The alliance negotiations with England and France
make sense only on the assumption that the Soviet statesmen
genuinely desired an alliance and discovered its impossibility
(for them as much as for others) only as they came to formulate
precise conditions. Similarly, the Soviet rulers had not thought
out what gains they were to demand from the Nazi-Soviet
pact; their full schedule was not ready until Molotov's visit

to Berlin in November 1940, and then it was too late—the
Soviet insistence on control of Finland, Bulgaria and the
Straits led Hitler to resolve on war. In fact, Constantinople
was the stake in the war of 1941 just as much as it had been
in the war of 1812. For Hitler, as for Napoleon. Constantinople
was the symbol for the mastery of the world. For Molotov,
as for Alexander I, the Straits were the one chink in Russia's
defensive armour; in Molotov's words, "England's historic
gateway for attack on the Soviet Union." The demand for
Soviet garrisons at the Straits was an old-fashioned way of
closing this gateway; nevertheless, it is difficult to think of
any other.

Beyond the *cordon sanitaire*, Soviet statesmen thought in
terms of the Balance of Power. There was sincerity in Stalin's
words: "A strong Germany is the absolute requisite for peace
in Europe, whence it follows that the Soviet Union is interested
in the existence of a strong Germany." This is the exact
counterpart of the attitude of the Western Powers, who had
welcomed a strong Germany as a barrier against Bolshevism.
Both sides burnt their fingers (and most of their bodies) with
this policy and now hesitate to renew it; hence the present
confusion of policy with regard to Germany. Still, the bidding
for German friendship must start soon; the only slender
hope of preventing it lies in a possible German weariness with
their warrior role. In 1939 Stalin counted on the French to
keep Germany occupied; he told Ribbentrop "that France
had an army worthy of consideration." Hence the indignation
with France which Stalin still showed in 1945: he complained
at Yalta that "France opened the gates to the enemy." The
French defended their own gates, though inadequately; the
gates which they opened to the enemy were the gates of Russia.
Soviet statesmen are not likely to fall victims again to the
illusion that France is a Great Power; and this lack of a Balance
of Power probably accounts for their apprehensions ever since
the end of the war. Those who could sit unmoved through
the endless harangues of Hitler, with his visions of a new
world order, will not easily be affected by American good
intentions; and, short of faith in these, it is difficult to
devise security except by means of the Balance of Power.

Maybe a more independent British policy since the war would have lessened Soviet anxieties; on the admittedly inadequate evidence of the German documents, however, Soviet opinion wrote off British power almost as much as French.

The German documents give a reminder of one factor often overlooked: Soviet policy is as intimately concerned with the Far East as with Europe. Here, too, the Soviet aim was a Balance of Power: Japan was to keep China in order and act as a buffer against America, yet not to conquer China nor be conquered by America. This Balance, too, has collapsed, though not so disastrously as the Balance in Europe; but, unless Communist China can be transformed into an adequate buffer, the Soviet Union will, one day, have to enter the competition for Japanese favour.

It may be objected that these considerations were valid only in the period of German and Japanese aggression; but the Soviet leaders do not distinguish between one capitalist State and another. Indeed, they found it easier to understand the Germans than the British and French or, subsequently, the Americans; and their anger at having been taken in by Hitler has made them resolve never to be taken in again. The Marxism which underlies their long-term policy reinforces these suspicions; their day-to-day policy would be much the same whether they were Marxists or not. After all, the Soviet Minister of Transport, also a Marxist, is concerned in day-to-day practice with the specifically "Russian" problems which spring from broad-gauge railways and a great land mass; the same is true of Soviet diplomacy. It is therefore a fair general deduction that the object of Soviet policy is security, based on a ring of buffer States and a Balance of Power beyond this ring.

There is, however, one economic factor, not specifically Marxist, since it was also characteristic of Tsarist policy in the days of the Franco-Russian alliance. The deepest force in Nazi-Soviet friendship was the exchange of raw materials and food-stuffs for machine-tools. This economic bargain was the essential preliminary to a political agreement on which Molotov insisted, and the Soviet outlook is not likely to have changed. Machine-tools would buy Soviet friendship on favourable economic and political terms for a long time to come. The peace and future of the world probably depends on whether anyone has machine-tools to offer and cares to offer them.

X

A VANISHED WORLD: THE MEMOIRS OF CORDELL HULL

CORDELL HULL was the last American Secretary of State before the flood. Words were his weapon and agreements the object of his policy, not the means by which it might be accomplished. He believed in a "normal" world of peaceful nations, trading freely without restrictions. When he entered the State Department in 1933 his sole aim was to secure the reduction of tariff barriers, and though when he left the State Department in 1944 the United States was at war in four continents he still thought in terms of Free Trade and the rule of international law.

These memoirs[1] contain almost three-quarters of a million words. Complacent and assertive, they use ten words to do the work of one and record even the number of telephones in the washroom attached to the Secretary's room. They come most alive in recording the internal disputes over policy-making; for, inside the Democratic party if not in the great world, Mr. Hull understood the problem of power. President Roosevelt was an improviser, listening to all kinds of advisers and then deciding on impulse; in fact, only the President's lack of interest in foreign affairs brought Mr. Hull to the State Department, and the economics of the New Deal were in direct contradiction with Mr. Hull's advocacy of lower tariffs. Still, Mr. Hull fought the unofficial advisers from Moley to Sumner Welles with persistence and success and even moderated some of Roosevelt's wilder inspirations.

There is nothing novel in the prolonged record of American dealings with the other American states or, for that matter, with Japan, though both gave Mr. Hull plenty of opportunity to ride the high horse of principle. By a curious contrast American dealings with Vichy France disregarded principle;

[1] *The Memoirs of Cordell Hull.* Two volumes.

and rebukes from Great Britain caused the principal topic of discussion in Anglo-American relations. Mr. Hull could never understand the emotional credit which de Gaulle had acquired by coming out on the British side in June 1940; on the other hand, he exaggerated the advantage gained from keeping in touch with Vichy. However, in spite of these disputes the controversy was in essence unreal; neither American favouring of de Gaulle nor British friendship with Vichy would have brought France back into the ranks of the Great Powers before the defeat of Germany. Indeed, the dispute only illustrates the general principle that Foreign Offices usually quarrel on dead issues and that in war-time their activities have little or no effect on the course of the struggle.

Anglo-American dealings over Germany are of greater interest. It is curious to learn that as late as August 24, 1939, British appeasers did not think all lost. Sir Horace Wilson, described as "of the British Foreign Office," "saw no way of escape except for the Poles to express their willingness to negotiate, and this was where pressure should be applied. The British, however, were not in a position to apply such pressure strongly, but if anything were to be done it must be done at once." The advice was not accepted.

Later, when America had entered the war, Roosevelt devised his own German policy. Thus "unconditional surrender" was his private invention at Casablanca, and he held to it in spite of the protests of the State Department, of General Eisenhower and of the British and Soviet Governments. He eagerly accepted the Morgenthau plan for "pastoralizing" Germany when it was presented to him at Quebec in September 1944. According to these memoirs Mr. Churchill at first indignantly rejected the plan, because "England would be chained to a dead body." However, Morgenthau won over Lord Cherwell with the argument that "Britain would acquire many of Germany's iron and steel markets and eliminate a dangerous competitor," and the Foreign Office, which had also opposed the scheme, was lured by Morgenthau's offer of a six-and-a-half-billion-dollar credit. Mr. Churchill then drafted a document embodying the scheme, and it was

initialled by him and the President on September 15. Back in
Washington Roosevelt defended it mainly for the advantage
it was supposed to offer Great Britain. He said, "The real
hub of the situation is to keep Britain from going into complete
bankruptcy at the end of the war." And again: "I just cannot
go along with the idea of seeing the British Empire collapse
financially and Germany at the same time building up a
potential rearmament machine to make another war possible
in twenty years." However, a week or two later the President
"said that he had no idea how he could have initialled the
memorandum."

By 1944 Roosevelt had come to think in terms of a four-
Power establishment to police the world. The four Powers
were to be the United States, Britain, Russia and China;
"all other nations, including France, were to be disarmed."
Each of the four Powers was to be dominant in its own region,
and they were to be kept on good terms by Roosevelt's influence with Churchill, Chiang Kai-shek and "Uncle Joe."
This project was never given practical application. The State
Department successfully resisted any recognition of Russia's
1940 frontiers in the Anglo-Soviet treaty; and Mr. Hull
always objected to anything which derogated from his handi-
work, the United Nations. Roosevelt, however, agreed that
Great Britain "should play the cards" in the Near East.

In 1943 Churchill argued for an invasion of the Balkans,
partly to keep Russia out, partly to avoid heavy British
casualties in a campaign across the Channel. "Britain would
never recover from it and would be so weakened that the
Soviet Union would inevitably dominate the European
continent." Roosevelt insisted on the Normandy campaign
on military grounds. The British then made the best of a bad
job and in 1944 proposed a temporary division of the Balkans
for war purposes—Rumania to Russia and Greece to England.
The State Department again resisted strenuously, but Roosevelt agreed to a three-month experiment on June 12, 1944,
without informing Mr. Hull; and by the autumn England
and Russia were dividing the Balkans in terms of percentages
(Yugoslavia was to be divided fifty-fifty). Here England had
negotiated towards Russia without consulting America until

the last moment; in regard to Poland, Roosevelt worked for a settlement with Russia without consulting England. He refused, indeed, to commit himself to any specific frontier; here, too, he hoped for solution by his own particular method of good-fellowship, followed by improvisation.

Both Roosevelt and Mr. Hull persistently avoided commitments even in war-time, except for the commitment to the vague phrases of the United Nations. Thus they would not even agree to guarantee the Portuguese colonies; the most they would do was to promise to "respect" them, and this promise was more than the British or French got for their Empires. In fact, both Roosevelt and Mr. Hull, in their different ways, supposed that American entanglement in world politics was temporary. When "normal" conditions returned, Mr. Hull counted on an improved Wilsonian system and Roosevelt on his personal contacts with the rulers of the Great Powers. Neither envisaged a policy leading to permanent military commitments and continuing economic action.

XI

THE AUSTRIAN ILLUSION

THE "state of war" with Austria has come to an end; and the British Government has been at pains to stress its friendship with "Independent Austria." An Austria, truly independent of Germany, offers great attractions. It bars the way against German aggression in central Europe; it provides a centre for economic and political co-operation between the neighbouring countries; merely by existing, it reduces the total of Germans in Europe by six or seven million. The Austrian republic in the nineteen-twenties had added advantages. Its enlightened social services and constructive Labour movement captured the affections of the British Labour party, as did no other country in Europe; at the same time, the musty charm of its decayed aristocracy and its ski-instructors, disguised as Tyrolese peasants, appealed to the British upper classes. Politically, culturally and socially, no country was so popular in England. It would be dangerous if this affection, so skilfully built up by the Austrians, was used as the foundation for political illusions. It is one thing to say, as Palacky did: "If Austria did not exist, it would be necessary to invent it"; for Palacky referred to the great Habsburg monarchy, a going concern. It is quite another thing to say: "Though Austria does not exist, it will be quite easy to invent it—and indeed we will pretend that we have already done so." Yet this is, in different forms, the policy of all the Great Powers.

The fragment of German territory called Austria has no roots in history, no support in the feeling of its people, no record even of resistance to Nazi rule. It was part of the old German Reich (the Holy Roman Empire of the German Nation) from beginning to end; and for many centuries the ruler of Austria was also German Emperor. When the Austrians were excluded from Germany in 1866, this was not their doing: it was the result of Austria's defeat at the

hands of Bismarck. The Austrians remained Germans—
German in speech, German in culture, German in political
allegiance. To describe them as "Austrians" gives them a
false historical background. Every subject of the Habsburg
Monarchy was an "Austrian"—Czechs, Poles and Slovenes
as much as Germans. Historically, the only other sense which
could be attached to the word "Austrian" would be an inhabitant of Lower or Upper Austria, a provincial definition
of no real weight. The present use of the word "Austrian,"
repudiating the historical definition, means: "an inhabitant
of one of the six German provinces of the Habsburg Monarchy
which were left over when the rest of the Monarchy broke
away to form national states."

This definition distinguishes in two ways. The Austrians
are different from other subjects of the Habsburgs in being
Germans; they are different from other Germans in having
been subjects of the Habsburgs. Of these two differences the
first is essential. It remains true with the passage of time. Since
there are now no dynasties in Germany, nor have been since
1918, the second difference is trivial. This was accepted by
the founders of "Austria" in 1918. What they intended to
create was not an independent state, but "German-Austria,"
member of a democratic German republic. They demanded
self-determination, not for the "Austrians," but for the
Germans of Austria and they included in this the German
inhabitants of Bohemia and Moravia. Thus Hitler, who got
his anti-Semitism and German nationalism from the German
nationalists in the Habsburg Empire, got the programme of
dismembering Czechoslovakia from the Social Democrats of
Vienna in 1918. "German-Austria" remained separate from
the German Reich, not from the will of her people, but from
the order of the victorious allies; and this severance was
regarded by Germans, both in Austria and in the Reich, as
the gravest injustice of the peace settlement of 1919. As
indeed it was, if self-determination had been truly its guiding
principle.

Independent Austria never repudiated its German character or allegiance. Parties in Austria often opposed various
political trends in Germany, but not more so than many

M

Germans of the Reich did themselves. In the 'twenties the Austrian Clericals disliked German Social Democracy; in the 'thirties the Austrian Socialists disliked German National Socialism. This did not make them the less German. Austria is often described as having been "occupied" or "conquered" by Hitler. When Hitler entered Vienna in 1938, he was welcomed by wilder and more enthusiastic crowds than Vienna had ever known. Was Hitler welcomed by cheering crowds in Prague? in Warsaw? in Rotterdam? in Paris? in Belgrade? in Stalingrad? And among those who welcomed the completion of national unity was Karl Renner, now President of independent Austria. The Austrian republic was "German" also in deeds: it continued the campaign against the Slovenes in Carinthia which had been begun by the German Nationalists before 1918. In fact, Austrian rule, in this way, surpassed Hitler's. The Austrian census, taken in 1934, allowed the existence of only 26,122 Slovenes. The Nazi census, taken in 1939, acknowledged 45,000. It is not surprising that in 1945 the Nazi Gauleiter handed over Carinthia voluntarily to a Social Democrat. This new government announced: "It considers its first task to be the preservation of a free and indivisible Carinthia."

No one disputes that many Austrians are democratically minded; so are many Germans. In fact, the Reich Germans have a much more creditable record of resistance to Hitler. But, democratic or not, the Austrians remain German in national loyalty. The only pure Austrians were the Jews of Vienna; and they have been exterminated. The Communists claim to be pure Austrians; hence their unpopularity in Austria. The solution of the Austrian problem lies in Germany; and not the other way round. When (if ever) there is a peaceful, democratic Germany, Austria will be a contented part of it. But Austria will never be an effective barrier against German nationalism.

XII

TRIESTE

In 1920, after the first German war, a frontier was established between Italy and Yugoslavia which offended against both national principles and economic sense.

British memories are short: a frontier which has existed for twenty years appears to us to have existed from time immemorial. It has long been forgotten that the frontier of 1920 had no other justification than that the Italians possessed superior force.

The territory in dispute is the area between the Italian frontier of 1914 and the Italian frontier of 1920, or roughly between the River Isonzo and the Julian Alps. Nowadays it is often described as Istria, though the former Austrian province of that name made up less than half of it.

The frontier of 1914 was also the old frontier between the Republic of Venice and the Holy Roman Empire, a frontier therefore of very long standing. It had been as well the national frontier between Italians and Slovenes, except for a handful of Slovenes (now about 50,000) west of the Isonzo, who were for centuries under Venetian, and since 1866 under Italian rule.

The frontier marked, that is, the point at which Slav incomers were arrested in the seventh century as they tried to come out on to the Italian plain; and it had thus remained a clear national frontier for over a thousand years.

The Slovenes are a distinct Slav people, not 2,000,000 all told, who have been settled for fifteen hundred years on both sides of the Julian Alps—the most western fragment of the southern Slavs. Not only was their territory without Italian inhabitants: it never had political connection with any Italian state. It was subdued from the north by German rulers and early in the sixteenth century became part of the family possessions of the House of Habsburg.

The Slovenes were once the people of the country. With the growth of towns they become the people of the countryside, in common with all other Slav peoples of Europe except the Poles.

The Germans and the Italians had a consolidated national territory for many centuries before they established a national state; even when the upper classes spoke French they did not cease to regard themselves as Germans or Italians. Beyond the German and Italian national boundaries events took a different course, though less completely with the Poles and Magyars than elsewhere.

Here, the national differences of to-day are the class differences of yesterday. The towns did not grow out of the country: they were the creation of foreign conquerors and of foreign merchants, German or Italian "islands" in a Slav sea. The peasants remained Slav; the trader, the shopkeeper, the artisan, in time the administrator and the professional man, spoke the language of the town and, whatever his racial origin, became German or Italian, Pole or Magyar. A prosperous lawyer would in this period no more continue to use the Slav tongue of his parents than he would continue to sleep over the stove.

Not a town in eastern Europe but bears witness to this rule. In 1815 two-thirds of the 60,000 inhabitants of Prague called themselves German. A century later, when the population had increased tenfold, only 20,000 Germans were counted.

Until 1880 the city council of Budapest transacted its business in German, since it was the body of the city merchants.

Riga was German; the towns of Transylvania were German; even the trading quarters of Constantinople had a German character.

Farther east the Poles played both parts in turn: in western Poland there were German towns in a Polish countryside, in eastern Poland there were Polish towns in a Ukrainian or Lithuanian countryside—Lvov the great example of the first, Vilna the great example of the second.

The territory of the Slovenes had two "colonizers." On the eastern side of the Julian Alps were the Germans, creating

towns with a German character at Ljubljana, Klagenfurt and
Maribor. On the Adriatic coast were the Italians. Two
centuries ago every fishing village and to outward view every
port from Venice to the southern tip of Greece appeared
Italian. These towns and villages were not inhabited by
Italians; but Italian was the language of administration and
trade, especially the language of maritime trade. Every seaman
spoke Italian as the uniform of his profession.

The peasants remained Slovene, as they had always been.
But until the beginning of the nineteenth century peasants
had no political existence; their nationality counted no more
than the nationality of their cattle. Even the French revolutionaries reckoned only with the educated and propertied
classes, reckoned, that is, with the towns. Hence, in 1815,
Istria seemed to be Italian, so far as it seemed to be anything
at all, as Dalmatia (where the Italians were not 5 per cent of
the population) seemed to be Italian, as Bohemia seemed to
be German, or as the Ukraine seemed to be Polish.

The great political event of the nineteenth century, which
is shaping the destinies of central and eastern Europe to the
present day, was the awakening of the peasant peoples. Towns
grew no longer slowly, but at breathless speed. Peasants
crowded in from the countryside too rapidly to be absorbed
into the urban nations. Their peasant dialects revived as
literary languages, and every peasant nation found intellectual
leaders.

This great process created, or re-created, the Czechs,
the Croats, the Slovaks, the Ukrainians—and the Slovenes.

In much of the area "colonized" by the Germans the
Slovenes asserted themselves without difficulty, and before the
end of the nineteenth century everybody recognized that
Carniola, the Slovene territory beyond the Julian Alps, was
inhabited almost exclusively by Slovenes.

It was the great misfortune of the Slovenes that, just before
their national awakening, there was created, on their national
territory, a great Mediterranean port, the greatest port in
southern Europe after Marseilles and Genoa, and that this
port was, quite without design, given an Italian character.
Even without Trieste the Italians would no doubt have striven

to maintain their superiority over the Slovenes, just as other "historic nations"—the Germans, the Poles, the Magyars—resisted national emancipation elsewhere and resist it to the present day. Without Trieste the Italian claims would have lacked plausibility and substance. Even Italian patriotism could not have been inflamed for the 20,000 Italians of Gorica, the westernmost part of this territory.

Trieste was an "artificial" town, a creation of the railway age and of German plans for European domination. Until the eighteen-forties it had been but an obscure fishing port of no trading importance. Its creator was Baron Bruck, a German from the Rhineland, and the first great advocate of the project which later became known as "Mitteleuropa"—the plan for bringing all Europe east of the Rhine under a single economic and political administration.

Bruck chose as the framework and trade name of this plan the Austrian Empire and the House of Habsburg. Only this mistake distinguished his aims from those of William II or Hitler.

Bruck built the first docks in Trieste and founded the first shipping lines. In 1848 he became Austrian Minister of Commerce and then made the Austrian Empire a single-tariff area with Trieste as the principal imperial outlet to the world.

These great schemes could never have been achieved before the age of railways, which freed central Europe from dependence on waterways and ended the monopoly of the Rhine, the Elbe and the Danube. So far as foreign trade was concerned, the Austrian railways were made to centre on Trieste. By the beginning of the twentieth century there was a double-track line to Salzburg and so to southern Germany; a double-track line to Vienna and so to Bohemia; a single-track line through the Julian Alps to the Slovene districts and Styria; a double-track line to Ljubljana which gave another route to Vienna and which, after the first German war, was extended to Zagreb and so tapped Croatia and western Hungary. But all this time no line of importance connected Trieste with Italy. Nor was this surprising—there was no real connection between Trieste and Italy.

Trieste fulfilled all Bruck's expectations. It became (to use the twentieth-century state names) the port of Austria, of Bavaria, of Hungary, of northern Yugoslavia and, to a considerable extent, of Czechoslovakia. Its trade range reached to western Rumania and to the Ukraine.

At the same time it would be a mistake to exaggerate the importance of the share of central European countries and to minimize the share of the territories which later became Yugoslav. One of the more subtle arguments of Italian apologists is to suggest that Trieste is the port of central Europe, not of Yugoslavia. The trade figures of 1913 do not bear this out. Of the total railway traffic of 2,800,000 (metric) tons more than a quarter (800,000) came from the lands inhabited by Slovenes: German-Austria and the Czech lands came next with about 600,000 tons each.

Austria and Czechoslovakia had also other outlets through the German North Sea ports. The Slovenes had only Trieste and when, after 1920, they were cut off from Trieste by the Italian frontier, they were ruined.

Two countries hardly figure in the statistics of 1913. One is Croatia. Croatia was severed from Trieste by the railway policy of the Hungarian Government (which controlled Croatia), designed to prevent any contact between Croatia and the Austrian part of the Austro-Hungarian Empire. Once a railway was built between Ljubljana and Zagreb, the capital of Croatia, as it was immediately after 1919, Croatia would have become a great user of Trieste, had not the Italian frontier barred the way. Then the Yugoslav share of the total would have reached at least 1,000,000 tons.

The other country which did not use Trieste was Italy. The Italian traffic with Trieste in 1913 was 85,000 tons, not 3 per cent of the total. The great port of Venice was more than adequate for Italian needs; and the Italians desired Trieste, not to use it themselves but to ruin it for the benefit of Venice, the merchants of which largely financed the political campaigns for its annexation and to prevent its use by others.

The trade statistics of 1913 can be thus summarized: Trieste was essential for the foreign trade of the Slovenes and of northern Croatia; it was useful for the foreign trade of

Austria and Czechoslovakia; it played no part whatsoever in the foreign trade of Italy. Thus, on economic grounds, Yugoslavia had the decisive claim to Trieste after the dissolution of the Habsburg Monarchy.

The great port traffic naturally brought with it industrial developments: not only shipbuilding but oil refineries, food industries and a great banking organization.

Trieste, not surprisingly, became the most important insurance centre in central Europe. It became, too, a cultural centre.

Just before 1914 it was inhabited by at least two writers of European importance, Svevo and James Joyce. It would be fanciful to find much of Trieste in *Ulysses*, though it must have been through Trieste that Bloom reached Dublin.

The writings of Svevo contain the full spirit of Trieste. Though written in Italian (by no means the purest Tuscan), they have nothing in common with Italian literature, but are manifestly the work of a fellow-countryman of Schnitzler. In other words they are works of "Austrian" literature, which merely happen to be written in Italian, as Schnitzler's happen to be written in German. Both writers felt as "Austrians" and, like many who felt so, both writers were Jews.

Trieste thus grew, *par excellence*, as an "Austrian" town, created for an Austrian Imperial purpose. It owed nothing to Italian effort. Like the Austrian Empire, it had no national character. It certainly did not serve, could never serve, any Italian economic need. So far as it served a national purpose, that purpose, again like the Austrian Empire, was German, not Italian.

But, for convenience and certainly not by national design, Italian was the maritime language of the Austrian Empire, a language inherited from the Republic of Venice, and this at a time when the Slovenes of the surrounding countryside were still a "submerged people." Therefore, when Trieste started on its career of greatness, it started as an Italian-speaking city, and remained predominantly so at the beginning of the twentieth century.

Thus its Italian language by no means meant that its

inhabitants were predominantly Italian by descent. The few thousand Italians who had made up its total population at the beginning of the century were soon swamped by a flood of immigrants from the neighbouring countryside, from the German lands farther north, and from the Levant. An Austrian inquiry of 1915 ascertained that more than half the population of Trieste was of Slovene descent, though two-thirds of the population considered themselves Italians.

A further element was of Croat descent. Add Germans and Jews (the most loyal of all Austrians) and there was little enough left of Italian blood. The majority of the population certainly called themselves Italian. But they did this rather as a mark of class distinction than out of Italian patriotism. The "Italian" lawyer, clerk, or merchant was asserting his distinction from the unskilled labourers who still admitted to being Slovenes; not in the least was he demanding separation from the Austrian Empire and inclusion in Italy. That would have been, and eventually was, his economic ruin.

The "Italians" voted together. But they did this rather as a party of middle-class interests, not on grounds of nationality. Even so, despite the majority who returned themselves as Italians (*i.e.* Italian-speakers) in the census, the Italian political party never won a majority of votes. The inhabitants of Trieste simply were not Italians. They were at that time Austrians, meaning by that controversial word subjects of the non-national Habsburg Empire, who spoke Italian only because they had to speak something. Through the traditions of Venetia and Mediterranean trade, at that time Italian seemed the obvious tongue.

The high-water mark of Italian preponderance in Trieste was reached about 1880, when Trieste had become a great port, and before the Slovenes began to recover their national consciousness. In 1880 only 22 per cent of the population was returned as Slovene.

Thereafter the tide turned. The "Italians" maintained a monopoly of commercial life, and practically a monopoly of schools and newspapers, the two weapons without which it is difficult to develop a national consciousness. Nevertheless Slovene nationalism asserted itself. At the last Austrian census, in 1910, 29 per cent of the population was returned as Slovene.

This increase owed something to further Slovene immigration from the countryside, but more to "conversion" of many who had previously been ashamed of their lower-class nationality. To be Slovene was at last becoming respectable, and since the majority of the population was indisputably Slovene or Croat by origin it was only a matter of time—had no outside force checked this development—before the majority of the population of Trieste would have reverted to its original nationality.

Austrian rule did not hold the balance perfectly even between South Slav and Italian. Like all imperial bureaucrats, the Austrian officials sympathized (perhaps unconsciously) with the wealthier upper-class Italianizers. Still, even so, had the Austrian Empire lasted for another generation, Trieste would have had a South Slav majority. Twenty-five years of Italian rule did not reduce the Slovene proportion to less than it was in 1910. The Italians, in fact, had to exhaust every weapon of national oppression merely to keep their numbers from declining.

The Austrian census of 1910 was the last free census, and also the last to take account of national character. It is therefore the only reliable basis on which to judge the national composition of these disputed areas.

It is not without faults. The census in the towns was taken by the municipal authorities, and these were still predominantly Italian.

The first count in Trieste found only 36,000 Slovenes; a revision made by the imperial authorities brought the number up to 56,000. In the other towns the figures were not revised. Further, the figures could give only the national balance as it existed in 1910; they could not allow for the process of Slovene awakening which was going on at an ever faster rate.

Grouping together all the Yugoslav territory acquired by Italy in 1920, and adding the 50,000 Slovenes already in Italy before 1914, there were altogether 538,331 Yugoslavs (Slovenes and Croats) and 354,000 Italians. A third of these

Italians lived in the two towns of Trieste and Gorica. The southern half of the Istrian peninsula was inhabited not by Slovenes but predominantly by Croats, kindred Yugoslavs who were passing through the same process of national awakening. Here, too, the Italians lived in the coastal towns, above all in Pola, a great harbour important not as a commercial port but as the base and construction centre of the Austrian Navy.

These figures give an unmistakable picture. The countryside was solidly Croat or Slovene. The towns were Italian "islands," which were gradually being submerged by the rising tide of the awakening peasant nation. As Prague and Brno became Czech; Bratislava, Slovak; Riga, Latvian; Posen, Polish; and Lvov, Ukrainian; so it seemed certain that Trieste would become Slovene.

The Slovenes had every quality of the other awakening people. Their only fault was to be overtaken, while still half-submerged, by the war of 1914–18.

Trieste was not a traditional object of Italian ambition. It was a recent creation and therefore counted for nothing in Italian tradition, unlike Venice—or even such Dalmatian towns as Split (Spalato). It had no economic significance for Italy. Moreover, the leaders of the Risorgimento, especially after 1848, saw that their success depended on preventing the Habsburg Empire from receiving German support. Anxious not to offend German sentiment (as against Austro-Hungarian), they consistently halted their ambitions at the frontier of the German world, and recognized that Trieste served German, not Italian needs. Even Mazzini, a man not usually influenced by practical considerations, declared the River Isonzo to be the natural frontier of Italy.

When the rising Kingdom of Italy acquired the province of Venetia from Austria in 1866 and occupied Rome (the Papal territory) in 1870, she had achieved full national unity. She could no longer live on an enthusiasm for national emancipation. The Italians had been promised great things from unification. Yet, in fact, Italy lacked all the qualities of a Great Power—except ambition.

Her politicians had exhausted themselves in achieving

unification. None of the younger men now possessed those
practical gifts in the international field which had distinguished
Cavour. Thus, in the eighteen-seventies, when Italy was torn
by popular discontent, by resistance to taxation and by
anarchist outbreaks, her rulers could think of no other solution
than artificially to return to the days of the Risorgimento and
to divert Italian feeling against the former Italian bogy—
Austrian rule.

The programme of this substitute-risorgimento, a very
inferior edition of the original, was a mixture of nationalist
claims and assertion of natural frontiers—the line of the Alps
and the emancipation of Italians still in Austria were demanded
together, though the two did not by any means coincide.

In fact the "natural frontier" involved the inclusion of
300,000 Germans and 500,000 South Slavs in Italy. Still,
this hardly mattered. The demand was not put forward as a
matter of serious politics. It was a safety valve for internal discontent. Trieste was the only place of any size in these coveted
areas.

Therefore Trieste became the symbol of the programme
as a whole, and for more than a generation the Trieste question
was kept alive so that riotous mobs should throw their stones
through the windows of the Austro-Hungarian Embassy
instead of through the windows of the Italian Home Office.

The agitation for Trieste did not prevent Italy's being for
more than thirty years (from 1882 to 1915) the ally of Austria-
Hungary in the Triple Alliance; just as membership of the
Triple Alliance did not prevent Italian politicians continuing
to proclaim the grievance of Trieste.

Italy would never have gone to war for the sake of Trieste;
yet when she went to war in 1915 Trieste inevitably provided
the excuse. Italy wished to take part in the first German war
in order to prove herself a Great Power, and she was anxious
to sell herself to the highest bidder. The Germans were ready
to bribe Italy with Habsburg territory, but they could not
agree to their own exclusion from the Adriatic: they offered
south Tyrol, but not Trieste.

England and France had no such hesitation. They believed
that the unbreakable German front in France could be turned

by an attack through Italy, and they were willing to pay almost any price, in terms of Habsburg territory, for Italy's entry into the war. They accepted Italy's claim to the "natural frontiers" of the Alps, and, knowing little or nothing of the national circumstances, hardly realized that they were agreeing to an act of national injustice. Even if they had, they would have argued that this was an inevitable sacrifice, worth making for the sake of a speedy victory.

Besides, the dissolution of Austria-Hungary was at this time no part of their programme. They supposed that the Habsburg Empire would continue to exist, even though in diminished form; and since the Habsburgs were now the agents of Germany, it was reasonable to transfer Trieste and Pola to Italy in order to cut Germany off from the Adriatic.

The Treaty of London of April 1915 concluded the bargain between Italy and the Western Powers. Italy was promised the line of the Alps and the northern part of Dalmatia.

The only point not included in Italy's gains was Fiume. This omission was not at all on grounds of justice. Fiume was technically part of Hungary; and as both the Allies and Italy cherished the illusion that a great Hungary would be a counterpoise against Germany, they left to this imaginary friend the outlet on the Adriatic.

England and France made, no doubt, a bad bargain; still, they acted with fairness according to their lights. The Italians had demanded the whole of the Dalmatian coast; but the Western Allies were loyal to Serbia and insisted that she should have her share in southern Dalmatia. Their fault was to fail to foresee the emergence of a state comprising all the South Slavs, though this was a fault shared by many of the South Slavs themselves.

At any rate, the Treaty of London paid to Italy an acceptable price and Italy entered the war with her claims to Trieste internationally recognized. The Treaty of London is the only legal basis for Italian rule in Trieste; and anyone who wishes to maintain this rule is, inescapably, an advocate of the Treaty of London. He is asserting not merely that Italy performed valuable services in the first German war, but that by these services (and despite her subsequent acts) she earned a reward which must be immutably preserved, whatever the injustices to others.

The Italians had called the war of 1859 "the war for Lombardy" and the war of 1866 "the war for Venice"; so in their attempt to recapture the glamorous days of the Risorgimento they called the first German war "*the war for Trieste*." But when the end of the war came in 1918 it was in circumstances very different from those envisaged in 1915. The Habsburg Empire dissolved and a state of the South Slavs sprang up over night.

But the Italians refused to abandon anything of their treaty rights. Italy was a nation of over 40,000,000 with a powerful army, ineffectual indeed against Germany or Austria-Hungary, but well-equipped by England and the United States; and England and France were bound to support her claims. Yugoslavia was newly created, without friends, her only force the Serb army which had paid a terrible price in the fighting against Austria-Hungary. Her first leaders, too, were Serbs who cared too little for the destinies of Slovenes and Croats in the remote north-west.

The Yugoslav cause was defended in the peace negotiations by President Wilson; he achieved nothing, except to destroy his popularity in Italy. The Great Powers would not coerce Italy, but shrank from themselves committing an act of national injustice. Therefore they passed by on the other side and left Italy and Yugoslavia to settle their frontier between themselves.

Yugoslavia was helpless and had to accept the Italian terms. The outcome was the Treaty of Rapallo of November 1920, which gave Italy all her demands except the coast of Dalmatia. This imperialistic treaty was not the work of Fascists. It was concluded when Italy was still a Liberal parliamentary country, and her Foreign Minister responsible for the Treaty was Count Sforza, a man of Liberal reputation.

This was not all. By the Treaty of Rapallo, Fiume was to become a Free City. Hardly had the treaty been signed, when an Italian adventurer, financed with Italian money and equipped with Italian arms, seized the city under the protection of the Italian Navy. Once more the Yugoslavs could do

nothing and in 1924 they acquiesced in the incorporation of
Fiume by Italy.

The fate of the Free City of Fiume is worth meditating by
those who welcome that Trieste has become a Free City in its
turn; and it is also worth meditating that the "legionaries"
who seized Fiume became thereafter the most violent and
successful agents of the Fascist *coup d'état*. Italy paid for the
enslavement of Fiume by being herself enslaved.

Thus Italy brought under her rule more than 600,000
Slovenes and Croats. The Italians rejected as an insult to their
national honour a proposal to give these South Slavs the
protection of the Minorities Treaty, though they were fulsome
in their assurances that their nationality would be respected.

Italy did not wait until the coming of Fascism to break
these assurances: they were never fulfilled even in the days
of constitutionalism. The guilt for the ill-treatment of the
Slovenes and Croats cannot be placed solely on Fascism: it
must be shared by Bonomi, by Count Sforza and by every
liberal parliamentarian.

Even were the future of Italian liberalism secure, it would
be small consolation to the Slovenes and Croats to return to
the days of 1920. Italian rule over these South Slavs had no
parallel in Europe until the worst days of the Nazi dictatorship.
The South Slavs were deprived of their schools; they were
deprived of their newspapers and books; they were not allowed
to use their language in public meetings or in the law courts;
the Slovene-speaking bishops and clergy were expelled, with
the connivance of the Vatican; even Slovene-speaking doctors
were forbidden. When it was urged on an Italian doctor that
his patients could no longer explain their symptoms to him,
he replied: "Nor can the cow explain its symptoms to the
veterinary surgeon."

Such was the Italian estimate of these peaceful, educated,
civilized Slav peasants. No Italian ever protested; no attempt
at improvement was ever made. Italians of all parties agreed
in the aim of exterminating the nationality of the Slovenes and
Croats under Italian rule.

This aim was not achieved. A people proves its right to
live by asserting its will to live; and no people has proved its

right better than the Slovenes west of the Julian Alps. The Italians were driven to ever-more terroristic methods and to great treason trials, one in 1930 and an even more brutal one in 1941.

The British public is fond of plebiscites. Here was a plebiscite continuing over more than twenty years, a permanent popular vote of which the result cannot be doubted. The Slovenes as a people refused to die; they refused to accept Italian rule.

Their opportunity came in 1940 when Italy entered the war on the side of Germany. At last the Slovenes could have allies. They then became, before the war had reached Yugoslavia proper, the allies of Great Britain when she had few others. They served as a rallying point for resistance throughout south-eastern Europe; and they became in time one of the strongest elements in the National Liberation Movement which grew up in Yugoslavia under Marshal Tito.

Thus the Slovenes do not ask to be liberated from Italy. They have liberated themselves. All they ask is not to be put forcibly back under Italian rule.

The Italians paid a heavy price for the possession of Trieste. Many of those who burnt Trade Union buildings and beat or murdered liberal Italian politicians had learnt their trade in Trieste, burning the headquarters of the Slovene national club and murdering Slovene spokesmen—with the approval of liberal Italians. Still worse, the possession of Trieste compelled Italy to a foreign policy of Imperialism, led her to revisionism and ultimately brought her to all the disasters of 1940 and the years that followed.

For Trieste was not, and never could be, an Italian port: it had neither trading connections with nor economic meaning for Italy. Under whatever national sovereignty, it remained the port of central Europe; it was inextricably bound up with its hinterland, as far north as Prague and as far east as Budapest. Formerly it had been the means by which German Imperialism advanced to the Adriatic; now it became the means by which Italian Imperialism tried to thrust itself into central Europe. Italian governments, even before Mussolini, manipulated the tariff charges of Trieste in order to compel the states of

central Europe to become Italian satellites. Yugoslavia and
Czechoslovakia would not degrade themselves in this way
and so were driven to use the ports of northern Germany,
until—too late—they discovered that they had given themselves an even worse master.

So grossly did the Italians abuse their control of Trieste
that goods produced five miles over the Yugoslav frontier
were exported by way of Hamburg. In Austria and Hungary,
however, there were reactionary or Fascist parties, which
rejected the settlement of 1919; and Italy held out the promise
of preferential treatment at Trieste as a means of helping
them to power. Horthy in Hungary, Dollfuss and Schuschnigg
in Austria, were Italian dependents; each destroyed democracy,
each preached revisionism, each opened the way to a new
German aggression. And the Italian control of Trieste was the
origin of their power.

Such are the facts about Trieste, and they are beyond
dispute. In the area as a whole the Yugoslavs are in an un-
challengeable majority, and even in Trieste the majority is not
Italian by origin. Trieste has no historical significance for
Italy. It has no economic importance for Italy. It has always
been exploited by Italy for imperialistic purposes and Italy
has proved herself unqualified to rule over peoples of other
nationalities.

There were four proposals before the negotiation of peace:

(i) The frontier could be left unchanged on condition
that Italy gave guarantees of good treatment of
the Slovenes;

(ii) The territory could be partitioned, giving the country
districts to Yugoslavia and leaving Trieste in
Italian hands;

(iii) The country districts could be given to Yugoslavia
and Trieste could be made a Free City; or

(iv) All the territory east of the Isonzo could be given to
Yugoslavia.

The principal argument in favour of the first course was
that the frontier established by the Treaty of Rapallo existed.
For the Yugoslavs to demand Trieste seemed somehow

N

grasping, in a way that it did not appear grasping of the Italians to desire to retain it.

This was not a very serious argument. It was more to the purpose to argue that the new democratic regime in Italy would start life under an impossible handicap if it were compelled to renounce territory for which Italy fought a great war and which a generation of Italians had been taught to regard as an integral part of Italy.

A plausible argument—though it would have applied with even more force to Alsace or Posen in 1919. Germany, too, had fought a great war for Alsace and this had been German for more than forty years, whereas Trieste has been Italian for only twenty-five. Yet the victorious Allies, of whom Italy was one, were unanimous in inflicting this handicap on the democratic German republic. Posen had been in German hands for more than a century and was universally regarded in Germany as German; yet the Allies were unanimous in restoring it to Poland.

The argument would appear equally fraudulent in the case of Trieste, were it not that Poland and France are historic countries, and the Slovenes are not—therefore it was possible to advocate national injustice at their expense in a way that would not be possible with the French or Poles. In any case, was it so certain that Italian national feeling was really so deeply bound up with the fate of Trieste? Certainly those elements which in essence had remained Fascist deplored the loss of Trieste, since this marked the end of Italy's imperialist plans in central Europe; but it is difficult to suppose that these elements carry much weight with democratic opinion.

Or rather they would not carry much weight if the present leaders of Italy genuinely set their faces against them. Italian feeling about Trieste is deliberately provoked by the new "democratic" journalists and politicians, as it was deliberately provoked by the liberal politicians of a previous generation. The purpose is the same: it is to unite Italy in some foreign quarrel and so distract attention from the terrible, and perhaps, insoluble domestic problems. Once it was the Austro-Hungarian embassy, now it is the Yugoslav mission, which provides the safety-valve for Italian political feeling.

Trieste is not the only object of Italian ambition which is endangered. Italy fought a war, with a great deal of patriotic enthusiasm, for Libya, which has been Italian for thirty years; and she fought a war, with quite unparalleled patriotic outbursts, for Abyssinia, which has been a principal element in Italian policy ever since 1889. If the Italian masses felt deeply about any foreign issue—and there is no evidence that they do—they would feel more deeply about Abyssinia, or even Libya, than about Trieste. Yet we are not told that the loss of Libya and Abyssinia will discredit the new democratic Italy beyond redemption.

And for a very simple reason: the Italian leaders know that in the present circumstances, their outcry will be ineffective where British interests are concerned. But they hope that the freedom of 500,000 Yugoslavs and the economic co-operation of central Europe is not a British interest.

One Italian argument in favour of retaining the 1920 frontier was, however, well founded, though it was no longer an argument which the Italians cared to use. When in 1919 the Italians pressed their claims to Trieste, they were repeatedly asked by President Wilson whether they would not be content with the possession of the city, allowing the country districts to go to Yugoslavia. The Italians always replied that he who possessed Trieste must possess its hinterland as far as the line of the Alps; and they were right.

To draw the frontier five miles behind the coast would create an impossible strategic position. It would condemn Trieste to starvation, since the city draws its food supplies from the whole of the hinterland.

The experiment of a city without hinterland was tried on a small scale at Zadar (Zara), a town on the Dalmatian coast which was allotted to Italy. This experiment was the ruin of Zadar: the inhabitants had to get their food supplies by sea from Italy; they could not even go for a country walk; and no peasants could come into the town to use the shops. Yet Zadar is little more than a village, Trieste a city of 250,000 inhabitants.

Such a frontier, ruinous to the inhabitants of the city, is also ruinous to the peasants of the hinterland. They lose the natural market for their products; they lack the enormous convenience of a great city at their doorstep; there are no secondary schools to which they can send their children; they have to put up with the very inferior amenities of petty village life.

Imagine what it would be like to live at St. Albans and be unable to visit London, or to live at Bury and be unable to visit Manchester. Yet St. Albans and Bury are sizeable towns: the Yugoslavs of Istria have none such. This argument was very well put by the Italians in 1919; it has now disappeared from their repertoire.

The argument of the last paragraph has anticipated the consideration of the second solution: solution by partition. This solution has a misleading appearance of fairness, attractive to the British public. The countryside is Slovene and Croat (Yugoslav), Trieste is—as to a majority—Italian, and is perhaps linked by an Italian-speaking coastal strip with Italy proper. This last is not an important consideration, since Trieste in practice is linked to Italy not by land but by sea.

Nevertheless, why not draw the frontier along the national line? This proposal was for more than twenty years violently rejected by all Italian writers, even the most enlightened, and it was repudiated by Count Sforza as late as the summer of 1944. But now the more skilful Italian propagandists realize that they must yield something, though they seek to yield as little as possible.

Salvemini, a man with a distinguished Liberal record, devised a most ingenious solution. He admitted that if the area be taken as a whole the Yugoslavs were in a considerable majority. Therefore, he said, let us not take it as a whole. Let us take the areas most distant from Trieste, the least valuable districts and the most backward; let us peel them off, as it were, until we have reduced the Yugoslavs from 600,000 to 300,000. Then the Italians would be in a majority and entitled to retain not only Trieste, but also territory inhabited by more than 250,000 Yugoslavs.

By a similar selection of certain wards of Glasgow or Liverpool, it could be proved that Glasgow and Liverpool ought to be ceded to Eire. Yet no one doubts that Glasgow is Scottish and Liverpool English.

And for a very simple reason: all over Europe, except in Istria, it has become an indisputable rule that the population of a territory must be taken as a whole and that a language "island" must follow the nationality of the surrounding countryside. Lvov, isolated from its countryside, has beyond dispute a Polish majority; yet with general approval it has become Ukrainian. The heart of Prague had, until recently, a German majority; yet it became Czech, with the approval of all but the Germans. In fact, as the historical analysis of the earlier part of this pamphlet showed, every town in eastern Europe was a foreign "island" in a peasant sea; but every "island" has had to accept the way of life imposed by the sea about it. Only the Slovenes are denied the advantage of this rule.

To leave Trieste, and no more, to Italy, has every conceivable disadvantage. It is economically ruinous. The Italians claim that by partition a national division has taken place and that they are therefore free from any obligations to the Slovene minority which remains.

For, while it was possible to partition this disputed area so as to leave no Italians under Yugoslav rule, it is not possible to partition so as to leave no Slovene under Italian rule; and, despite the silence of the Italian census figures, there are at least 60,000 Slovenes in Trieste alone.

Every friend of Italy hopes that Italian liberalism will have a rebirth, and in this hope keeps charitably silent about Italy's record during the twenty years between the wars. For this reason I have deliberately spent only a brief paragraph on the story of Italian terrorism and misrule over the Slovenes, though it is a story which could fill a book. But when Italians write as though it were unthinkable that Italians should ever be under Yugoslav rule, but reasonable that Slovenes should be under Italian rule, it is impossible not to recall the record of those twenty years. On that record there can be only one verdict: Italy, whether liberal or Fascist, cannot be entrusted with rule over non-Italian peoples.

Perhaps it is harsh to make too much of the historical

record; but it would be dishonest to pass it over. These things happened. They may be excused—though I can think of no excuse. But they cannot be ignored. Italian rule over the Slovenes (and over the Germans of the Tyrol) had no parallel in Europe, until the worst days of Hitler.

Let us, with the Italian propagandists, question the good faith of the new Yugoslav rulers; let us suppose that in a little while Yugoslavia will revert to the worst days of the dictatorship of King Alexander. Even in those days the 10,000 Italians of Dalmatia under Yugoslav rule had their own newspapers, and more schools than all the 600,000 Yugoslavs in Italy. Thus, the record of Yugoslavia at its worst is better than that of Italy at its best.

But even were we to turn our backs altogether on the past and to suppose that Signor Bonomi, Count Sforza and their liberal colleagues would behave in 1946 or 1947 in a totally different way from the way that Signor Bonomi, Count Sforza and their liberal colleagues behaved in 1920, the economic arguments against partition remain. The British and American public are not much concerned with these political disputes. For the sake of peace they are prepared to acquiesce in national injustice. But they desire that Trieste shall recover its old greatness and become again the port of central Europe.

For the sake of argument we may pretend that Italy will give up her imperialist plans in central Europe. But Trieste has no economic meaning for Italy except as an instrument for these economic plans; a truly pacific Italy will therefore inevitably neglect Trieste. Trieste is a great port; its docks and harbours cost money and need constant care. But Italy is a poor country and is likely to remain so. For very many years the Italian Minister of Transport will have a limited budget; and he would have in his charge four great ports—Naples, Genoa, Venice and Trieste.

The first three of these serve Italian needs and every penny spent on them will benefit Italy. Trieste does not serve Italy, and money spent on it would be merely a charitable contribution for the benefit of the states of central Europe. Will an impoverished Italy be anxious to make these gifts of charity? Is it indeed reasonable to expect her to do so? To leave Trieste

in Italian hands is to condemn Trieste to decay, to fetter the
economic development of Yugoslavia, and to compel both
Austria and Czechoslovakia to depend on the North Sea ports
of Germany.

Thus, the proposal to leave Trieste in Italian hands is
condemned on every ground. The third solution is to attempt
to devise some method of taking Trieste away from Italy
without giving it to Yugoslavia. This seems a strange ambition;
but the reason for it, though not consciously appreciated by
its authors, is easy to appreciate. It springs from the belief
that the Italians are civilized and that the Yugoslavs are not,
and that therefore Italians should not be put under Yugoslav
rule. In the popular mind, the Italians are still the heirs of
Dante and of the Renaissance; and the Yugoslavs are, as
Bismarck called them, "sheep stealers." No one can hold this
view who has ever been to Ljubljana or has lived among the
Slovenes. But few English people visit Ljubljana and many
visit Rome; and, when they visit Rome, they conveniently
forget that they are visiting the city of Mussolini.

If we pass the sponge of oblivion over the Italian record of
the last twenty years, we must also pass the sponge over the
record of the preceding centuries, which the Italians themselves have found it easy to forget. To talk as though the
Italians belong to western civilization and the Slovenes and
Croats do not is indeed to remain faithful to the spirit of the
British Prime Minister who supported German claims against
another "far-away people of whom we know nothing."

The only serious proposal which would keep the Yugoslavs out of Trieste was to make Trieste a Free City. This is
a very different thing from making Trieste a free port, a
proposal that is not in dispute. A free port merely implies
that goods passing to or from Czechoslovakia, Austria,
Hungary or other countries beyond Yugoslavia would not
have to pay Yugoslav customs dues; apart from any international obligations that were imposed, this would be imposed
by Yugoslav self-interest, since it would promote the prosperity
of Trieste.

Since even if Trieste does not go to Yugoslavia, Yugoslav
territory will intervene between Trieste and these countries;

exemption from Yugoslav customs dues will have to be arranged in any case.

A Free City is much more than a free port; it is an independent State, governing itself; perhaps under some international supervision. To make Trieste a Free City has certainly ensured that its Italian character will ·be preserved, since the Italians have a majority on the city council. It may ensure that Trieste will play its part as the outlet for central Europe.

But, since neither Italy nor Yugoslavia are willing to provide the money for its upkeep, it has to be subsidized by the Great Powers who imposed the solution. Does this also ensure the Slovene minority in the city their full national rights or that the Slovenes of the hinterland can develop their national culture in Trieste?

The answer is easy. If the city council is unchecked, there is no national equality. The immediate majority are Italians —the very men who took the lead in all the worst activities of Fascism. They are perfectly aware that, with fair play, the Slovenes will eventually acquire a majority, as they were already on the way to do before 1914. The Italians can hold their own only by forbidding Slovene schools, Slovene newspapers, and the use of Slovene in the law courts and public offices.

The international commission will, therefore, have constantly to intervene. If it insists on fair treatment for the Slovenes, there will be Italian riots in Trieste, and all over Italy as well; if it fails to insist, there will be Slovene riots in Trieste, and a violent outburst of feeling all over Yugoslavia.

Ultimately, the international commission, inadequately provided with armed support—or, probably, not provided with it at all—will despair, and Trieste will relapse into Italian hands. The Yugoslavs are the smaller State and will have to acquiesce, as Poland had to acquiesce in the German advance at Danzig.

But, no, Poland did not acquiesce. At the last moment she found backers among the Great Powers and resisted German demands. Is it likely that Yugoslavia will be without a backer among the Great Powers?

After all, we have a certain experience in how Free Cities

work. History may not be a good guide, but it is all we have; and in regard to Free Cities the experience of history is decisive. Two Free Cities were created after the first German war— Fiume and Danzig.

The severance of Fiume from Italy was not imposed upon Italy by the Great Powers, as the severance of Trieste from Italy was imposed by the Great Powers. It was proposed by the Italians themselves and contained in the Treaty of Rapallo, which Italy voluntarily signed with Yugoslavia. Yet, as soon as the Treaty had been signed, Italian filibusters seized Fiume, with the support of Italian warships; and the Italian Government threatened the Yugoslavs with war when they attempted to restore the settlement according to the Treaty which Italy herself had proposed.

In 1924, four years after the Treaty of Rapallo, Italy compelled Yugoslavia to tear up the Treaty and to agree to the Italian annexation of Fiume. Is it surprising that the position of Trieste as a Free City is regarded without enthusiasm by the Yugoslavs? They believe, and not without good grounds, that it is a method of keeping the door open for Italian claims until Italy is strong enough to enforce them.

But it may be said that the cases of Fiume and Trieste are not analogous: Fiume became a Free City by a voluntary act and its freedom depended solely on Italy's good faith, never a strong element in Italian policy. Trieste has been made a Free City by the Great Powers and its freedom will be maintained by them.

We have also had experience of this type of Free City. In fact, the friends of Italy in 1945 need simply to take out of the second-hand cupboard the arguments which were used against the Polish claims to Danzig in 1919. Danzig was said to be inhabited solely by Germans. This was true, a good deal truer than that Trieste is inhabited solely by Italians. Of Danzig's 360,000 inhabitants, less than 10,000 were Poles; within the city limits of Trieste there are at least 60,000 Slovenes, a third of the population, and since the Free City has been extended to include some of the immediate hinterland this proportion has been at least doubled.

It was said that German sentiment would be offended if

Germans were put under Polish rule, in fact, that it was impossible to put civilized Germans under the rule of the barbarous Poles. A great deal was made of Danzig's historic significance for Germany and of the cultural importance of Danzig for Germany; just as some now talk of the importance of Trieste for Italian culture and Italian history.

In both cases, this importance is imaginary, though in the case of Danzig there was perhaps a little excuse for it. It was asserted that Polish economic needs would be perfectly met by the creation of a Free City. And, finally, it was emphasized that the Free City would be under the guarantee of the League of Nations and that the Great Powers could be relied upon to defend it from either Polish or German encroachments.

Every schoolboy knows how these expectations were falsified. Danzig did not serve Polish economic needs. The Poles were compelled at enormous expense to build a harbour of their own. German sentiment was not satisfied with the position of Danzig as a Free City; rather it regarded this position as a standing invitation to agitate for the return of Danzig to Germany.

After all, if the Great Powers had refused to give Danzig to Poland in 1919 when Germany was prostrate, they would surely not refuse it to Germany when she was again powerful. The League of Nations proved impotent to protect the rights either of Poland or of the democratic German minority in Danzig.

The Great Powers made feeble attempts not to intervene but to mediate. Soon they wearied even of this and left Poland to negotiate directly with Germany—as Yugoslavia was left to negotiate directly with Italy in 1920. Danzig's final gift to mankind was to provide an excuse for the most destructive war in history, in which both the Soviet Union and the British Empire only just escaped total defeat. And this is the experiment which the friends of Italy have repeated at Trieste!

The experiment will have the same results. Italian sentiment will not be satisfied with the status of a Free City; it will accept the invitation to agitate for the return of Trieste to Italy. The City Council, with its Italian majority, will not seek to promote Yugoslav commerce. Still more—a cause of quarrel which did not exist at Danzig—it will neglect the Slovene schools, or, more probably, attempt to close them.

To make Trieste a Free City has no other purpose than to hold the door open for the reassertion of Italian claims at a time when Italy will be better equipped to enforce them than she is now. The Free City idea is a post-dated cheque with which to buy off the Yugoslavs; but when, in a few years' time, they present it to the World Security Organization, it will be returned marked "*refer to drawer*." And where then will be the drawers, the unpractical idealists of England and America?

They will be explaining away, or ignoring, the Italian treatment of the Slovenes, declaring that, after all, civilized Italians cannot be put under the rule of barbarous Slavs, and denouncing, as harsh and unjust, the very peace settlement which, it was claimed, would satisfy Italian opinion!

Thus, by a process of elimination, we are left with the fourth solution: of applying in this disputed territory the rule which has been accepted everywhere else in Europe and determining its destiny *according to the predominant nationality of the whole*. The frontier should be drawn where the Slovene countryside ends and the Italian countryside begins, a national frontier which has not changed for a thousand years; and the towns should share the destiny of the countryside.

This would undoubtedly be the best economic solution. Trieste would be the only great port in Yugoslav hands, and the Yugoslav Minister of Transport would make it his principal concern. Fiume, its only rival, has only a single-track line with a very steep gradient to the main trunk line through Zagreb and, owing to natural obstacles, can never be a port on the same scale; it would never have been created at all, except for the Hungarian desire to have a port not under the control of Vienna.

Moreover, co-operation with the other states of central Europe must be an essential element in Yugoslav policy; therefore, as a matter of Yugoslav interest, everything will be done to make Trieste the major port of Czechoslovakia, Hungary and Austria. This would have a profound political effect, and one which it is a British interest to promote.

When Trieste was in Italian hands, it was used as a political weapon to divide central Europe and to compel Austria and Hungary to follow a policy hostile to Czechoslovakia and Hungary. If Trieste were in Yugoslav hands, it would also be used as a political weapon, but to compel Austria and Hungary to co-operate with Czechoslovakia and Yugoslavia.

This would be regretted only by the friends of Archduke Otto of Habsburg and of Admiral Horthy, and it is difficult to believe that they are deserving of sympathy.

There remains the national question. Would not the Yugoslavs inflict on the Italian inhabitants of Trieste all the injustices which the Italians have inflicted on the Slovenes and Croats? There are strong grounds for believing that they would not.

In the first place, Yugoslavia is not, as Italy is, a national state. It is a federal state, containing at least five distinct nationalities, and comprising six federative units. The present Yugoslavia has far more in common with the old non-national Habsburg Empire than with a national state such as Italy; and though there are likely to be national disputes in the future—as there should be in any healthy country—no one nationality will predominate. Besides, the Slovenes are less than 2,000,000, of a total Yugoslav population of 16,000,000, so even the idea of a Slovene domination is out of the question.

There is a second, and more decisive, argument. The Italian majority in Trieste is artificial. It can be maintained only by denying to the Slovenes their national rights, and when in the old days of the Habsburg empire the Slovenes enjoyed something like fair play, the Italian majority was dwindling rapidly. The Italians had to close the Slovene schools in order to keep their position. The Slovenes will only have to open their schools in order to start catching up again. It will not be necessary for them to close the Italian schools.

Once the Slovenes are allowed to use their own language in the law courts and public offices, once they can send their children to Slovene schools, once Slovene books and newspapers can circulate freely, thousands who have called them-

selves Italians will revert to their nationality of origin. Moreover, when Trieste again becomes a great port—which it can
never be under Italy—there will be a great demand for labour,
and Slovenes will crowd in from the neighbouring countryside.

The Slovenes will become a majority, probably within a
generation; but they will become the majority by a natural
process. To do so they will not need to employ the weapon of
national persecution. This process has taken place, or is taking
place, in every town of eastern Europe; it can take place just
as easily in Trieste.

The reader will observe that I have conducted this argument on the most cynical basis. I have not attempted to make
out that the Italians are, by nature, intolerant and chauvinistic
or that the Slovenes are, by nature, tolerant and pacific.
Though I think that the evidence would justify such an
attempt, we must apply the same measure to both sides.
Either we assume (as Italian propagandists do) that the
Yugoslavs will remain bellicose and intolerant—in which
case we must assume the same of the Italians. Or we assume,
as Italian propagandists do, that the new Italy will behave
in an entirely different way from the old—in which case we
must assume the same of the Yugoslavs.

But it is an outrageous assumption to suppose that the
Yugoslavs, who have been our allies, will possess all the vices
of the old Italy; and that the Italians, who have been our
enemies, will possess more virtues than any people has ever
shown.

If both nations remain in the future what they have been
in the past, then Trieste should be Yugoslav, for the Italians
have shown themselves unfit to rule over Slovenes, whereas
the Yugoslavs are likely to treat the Italian minority con-
siderately, if only as a matter of self-interest.

If both nations live up to the fine promises of the present,
then Trieste should be Yugoslav; since an Italy which had
genuinely abandoned imperialist ambitions would not desire
to retain Trieste, and the Italians in Trieste would be more
prosperous under Yugoslav rule than if they remained in
Italy.

If the Italians live up to all their fine promises and the

Yugoslavs to none of theirs—then and then only, Trieste should indeed be Italian—but Malta, Tobruk and Addis Ababa should be Italian as well!

The liberal Press in England was shocked that the Yugoslavs insisted on liberating Istria themselves, instead of waiting for the decision of a peace conference; from this the worst conclusions were drawn.

Memories, especially British memories, are short. But the Yugoslavs had not forgotten that they awaited the decision of a peace conference in 1919. In 1919 they went to Paris with clean hands and their claims were supported by the President of the United States; they came away from Paris with their hands empty.

Italian rule in Trieste rested on the same right as German rule in Prague, in Warsaw, in Paris, or in the Channel Isles —the right of conquest; the only difference is that the Yugoslavs were compelled to agree to their temporary defeat by the Treaty of Rapallo.

Thus, too, the Soviet Union was compelled to acknowledge the loss of the western Ukraine and of western White Russia to the Poles by the Treaty of Riga in 1921. But that did not prevent the Russians liberating these territories—with the approval of Great Britain and the United States.

What sanction and authority does the Treaty of Rapallo possess which the Treaty of Riga did not possess? What claim has the Ukraine to Lvov which Yugoslavia does not possess to Trieste? The Yugoslavs have not attempted to seize any territory which is either ethnically or historically Italian. They have simply claimed territory in which there is an indisputable Yugoslav majority and of which they were robbed by violence in 1920.

They did no more than the Czechs did in liberating all Czechoslovakia to the pre-Munich frontiers, without waiting for the verdict of an international conference. Yet the Munich settlement was an international arrangement, agreed to by England and France, while the Treaty of Rapallo was imposed upon Yugoslavia by Italy without the consent of any third party.

It was strange political mathematics to suppose that it is

right in 1945 to repudiate an agreement imposed by force in 1938, but wrong to repudiate an agreement imposed by force in 1924. Fourteen years was indeed a short period in which to turn wrong into right.

Postscript—(1949)

This essay was written as a pamphlet in 1945 at the request of the Yugoslav Government. It originally ended with the plea that to recognize Slovene claims to Trieste would strengthen good relations between East and West. This ending was removed at Yugoslav suggestion; it was not for them, they said, to advise on the relations of the Great Powers. At the time I supposed this to be an exaggerated demonstration of Yugoslav independence. Now I know better. The only chance for the Yugoslavs was to base their claim on historic and national justice; Soviet backing, far from being a help to them, drove the other Great Powers into uncompromising opposition. The question of Trieste and of Istria was conducted purely as a trial of strength. The Russians backed Yugoslavia solely in order to show that they could protect their satellites; the others opposed Yugoslav claims in order to weaken the Communists in Italy and in order "to keep Russia off the Adriatic." A glance at the map would have shown that, if Russia and Yugoslavia were indeed the same (which has proved to be far from being the case), then Russia was on the Adriatic already—at Rijeka (Fiume) and Pola, to say nothing of Split and the bay of Kotor. In these circumstances, though the Slovenes were robbed of their historic city and Yugoslavia of her natural outlet, it was a great victory to have secured even the establishment of Trieste as a Free City.

The policy of the Western Powers was calculated to force Yugoslavia even more firmly into the arms of Russia; only the fantastic pride of the Yugoslavs defeated this outcome. Though I thought poorly of western policy, I confess that it never occurred to me that, within two years of signing the treaty of peace, the Western Powers Would propose to hand over the Free City to Italy. A strange argument : since

Trieste cut off from its hinterland proved unworkable, a way out was to be found by cutting it off still more completely. And since Fascism is reviving in Italy, it should be countered by granting the demands which the Fascists make. In my naïve view the wisest course for a Great Power, even in its own interest, is to follow the path of right and justice; this view does not seem to be held by others. The Western Powers, far from welcoming Yugoslav independence of Russia, seek only to demonstrate Yugoslav dependence on themselves; and now demand that Yugoslavia should abandon Trieste even as a Free City. Those who did not shrink from the roars of Marshal Stalin are not likely to be overawed by Mr. Bevin; and the Yugoslavs will disappoint the Western Powers as much as, previously, they disappointed the Kremlin.

XIII

TITO AND STALIN

THERE was a time when the great of this world—kings and emperors—conducted their affairs in secret. They met, wrote each other letters, made their decisions; and historians discovered the explanation of events only fifty or a hundred years afterwards. Nowadays the background of events is not kept long in cold storage. Even the private letters of the great—the most personal expression of their policy—even these are soon made public. Mr. Churchill publishes his own letters, Mr. Sherwood publishes the letters of President Roosevelt; you can read—though not in English—the letters exchanged between Hitler and Mussolini. Only one of the great keeps silent, aloof and mysterious as the Tsars, his predecessors; we know little of the letter-writing style of Joseph Stalin. Indeed we know little of Stalin's personality at all: a few works of Bolshevik theory, arid and heavy, and speeches still more impersonal—without literary grace, repeating a few simple formulas with crushing weight—after reading these Stalin appears more a myth than a man, an eastern idol of solid steel. Curiosity about Stalin would be ground enough to welcome the letters exchanged between Tito and Stalin in March and May of 1948. The impersonal tone is still kept up. Tito and Kardelj, his principal assistant, sign their letters and address them to Stalin and Molotov: the Soviet letters come back signed only "Central Committee of the Communist Party of the Soviet Union"—the voice of an oracle or of a god. All the same, a human being can be seen dimly through the incense—the same human being of whom Lenin said, just before his death, that he was too rude to remain Secretary of the Communist party; the old Bolshevik who has survived all his original colleagues, having indeed eliminated them by years of patient intrigue; the man who can brook no rival near the throne.

o

No one would offer the Tito-Stalin letters as a literary pleasure. Beneath a cover of clumsy Marxist phrases, they exchange accusation and abuse. Your answers are untrue and utterly unsatisfactory, says Stalin, you are Trotskyites and Mensheviks. Tito replies: your accusations are surprising and insulting. This rough bludgeoning is a commonplace of Communist style, a first rumble of the excommunication which is followed, inside Russia, by the trial and the firing-squad, outside Russia by expulsion from the party. The Comintern had plenty of trouble with heretics from its earliest years, particularly in the German Communist party, the strongest party of the twenties. Even our own Communist, Mr. Pollitt, went off the rails in 1939 at the beginning of the second German war. All the previous excommunications have worked: the sinners have either repented or been broken. Tito has not repented. Far from repenting, he has followed his letters with further acts of defiance. For instance, there is the Yugoslav pamphlet "Unprincipled and unjust accusations against the Yugoslav Communist party." It states: "no one is disputing the authority of the Soviet Communist party, no one in his right mind can deny its past and present role. But authority is not everything—truth is above authority." Then, even more daring, the direct challenge to Stalin himself: "Stalin is the greatest living authority . . . in the democratic world [that is, in the Communist world]. But in this dispute between the Yugoslav Communist party and the Soviet-Communist party, right is not on his side but on the side of the Yugoslav Communist party." Tito has not been broken either. He has held his own as ruler of Yugoslavia and leader of the Yugoslav Communist party—apparently more popular than ever. It is the first successful revolt inside the body of Communism, the only dynamic religion of our time.

Some people have suggested that the quarrel between Tito and Stalin is a put-up job, though it is difficult to see what it is put up for—presumably in some way Tito was to be a Trojan Horse in the western world. This seems to me a journalistic explanation. A journalist always believes a sensational story and seeks a complicated superficial explanation; a historian believes few stories and seeks a simple profound explanation. Neither attitude is always right; but nine times out of ten the elaborate plot, the intrigue, the mystery is an invention of the outside observer. Human affairs are much more obvious, drabber, cruder, than the journalist makes out. In the Tito affair, neither side could risk staging a put-up quarrel—the danger of that kind of quarrel is that it may turn into a real one. The idea of Communists challenging the authority of Stalin and of the Cominform is much too subversive to be played with. This theory of the "put-up job" is the work of those who believe that when a man becomes a Communist he ceases to be a human being. The Tito affair is the decisive proof that they are wrong.

On the other side are those—particularly high-minded Left-wingers in this country—who treat the dispute as a profound conflict over serious economic issues—how to handle the peasants, whether the Yugoslav Five-Year plan is too ambitious and so on. Charges of favouring the "kulak," the rich peasant, and of making a muddle of industry are certainly made in Stalin's letters to Tito; these charges are the small-change of Communist controversy. All the "mistakes" which Tito is charged with (and many more) have been made in the neighbouring countries — Hungary, Rumania or Bulgaria. The Communists of these countries have escaped excommunication because they always respond to the crack of Stalin's whip. Similar charges were made years ago in the disputes within Russia by which Stalin eliminated his old colleagues—sometimes they were too "Left," sometimes they were too "Right." After all, once you accept the position that Stalin is always right, it is very easy to show that anyone else is wrong. Trotsky, for instance, was driven out of Russia— a great blunder on Stalin's part, by the way, to let Trotsky slip through his fingers, but you have to learn every job, even the job of a secular Pope—Trotsky was condemned for advocating the planning of industry; a few years later Bucharin and his associates were condemned and shot for being doubtful about the planning of industry. The reason why people in the west fall for this delusion that the economic dispute is the essential issue is quite simple: Socialist parties in the west are organizations for welfare, for them the economic issues are truly essential, and so western Socialists think the same is true of Communist parties. But Communist parties are not organizations for welfare: they are organizations for power. Communists do not care at all about the immediate welfare of the people—that is why, for instance, they were the most violent resisters of the Germans, they did not care how many people were killed in reprisal. The primary object of Communist parties is to get power, by any means. Power is an end in itself; but they also want power in order to establish a Communist community, a secular heaven, heaven on earth, and they do not mind if they sacrifice an entire generation in the process.

Communism is the only dynamic religion of our time. It is not a particular way of arranging economic life, a thing about which you can argue; and the Communist parties are not political parties in the ordinary sense. Communism is a creed held by millions of people all over the world; in fact, it is the only living religion which can command fanaticism on a mass scale. A man is not won over to Communism by argument: he is converted, "saved," and from that moment his mind is closed to reason. He is ready to do whatever authority prescribes. That supreme authority used to be the Comintern, a more or less impersonal body with even some show of election. The Comintern was abolished in 1943, and many people hailed this as the end of international Communism; the Bolsheviks, they thought, had become straight Russian patriots. It occurred to me that there might be a more obvious explanation: maybe Stalin abolished the Comintern for the same reason as the Popes undermined the General Councils of the early Christian church—to concentrate authority in his own hands. At any rate, whether designed or not, 'that has been the result: Stalin personifies Communism and you can't be a Communist without believing that Stalin is always right. When Stalin speaks, he is inspired, he is the Vicar of Marx, Lenin, and of himself on earth. The Cominform is a very thin cloak for Stalinist authority. This is shown in the Cominform resolution excommunicating Tito and the Yugoslavs or, as it is called, putting them "outside the family of the brotherly Communist parties." Nice brothers

who accuse Tito of "a purely Turkish, terrorist régime."
Apart from this fraternal phrase, the resolution is merely a
hotch-potch of Stalin's earlier letters, a hotch-potch which
cannot be understood without referring back to the original
text.

Communism is a great secular religion; it aspires to be
a universal church and offers to everyone the choice only of
conversion or extermination—just like Islam or the Roman
Church in its days of supreme power. It is a great mistake to
suppose that these fanatical religions can be beaten by tolerance
and sympathy. Nothing succeeds like persecution: look at
the victory of the Inquisition over the Albigensians or in
Spain. In most of history Gresham's law operates: the bad
drives out the good. The periods of peace and decency—the
Augustan age in Rome or the late nineteenth century in
Europe—are freak periods, few and far between. The Roman
philosophers were tolerant, civilized, cultured; but they were
routed by the early Christians. The universal religions fail
only when they break down from within—either they are
rotted by ease and wealth—it becomes too much trouble to
go on exterminating and persecuting—or a believer revolts
against "authority," against the Caliph or the Pope. I used
to be inclined to think that Communism would lose its force
only when the Communist leaders began to enjoy the fruits
of power—to put wealth before power in fact; and that is a
process which takes generations, if not centuries. But maybe
there is something in the revolt from within. After all, it was
Luther, a monk in rebellion, and not some pagan of the
Renaissance, who brought down Rome. Luther came just at
the right time: he expressed the German national resentment
against foreign authority and knocked the bottom out of the
universal Church. The technical form of his heresy did not
matter; the essential thing was that he was under the protection
of the German princes and so beyond the reach of the arm of
the Inquisition. Otherwise Rome would never have argued
with him; it would have blotted him out.

Tito, too, is the revolt from within; and he is the one
Communist in the world out of range of the Soviet secret
police. For a very simple reason: he has a secret police of his

own. Tito is the only Communist ruler who has made himself.
Certainly he is "Moscow-trained," chateau-bottled, as it were.
But he has been away from Moscow for a long time, and the
other Yugoslav leaders have hardly been in Moscow at all.
Tito is the only Communist ruler who stayed in his own
country all through the war and did not liberate it—in his
own phrase—by returning afterwards in an aeroplane smoking
a pipe. Yugoslavia was cut off from Russia all through the
war and made war in its own way. The Yugoslav Communists
claim a unique war-record. Others resisted the Germans;
they liberated their country. It is this which lies behind their
present revolt. They say: "since we made revolution in our
own way, why should we not head for Socialism along our
own path?" The Russians, too, used to make a great thing of
Yugoslav achievements: now they deny that there was anything
special in them. I had a brush myself with the Russian writer
Fadeyev when he left Yugoslavia out of the list of countries
who resisted the Germans; as the Yugoslav pamphlet says,
"an English reactionary called his attention to the fact that
Yugoslavia also fought." Stalin himself, in his letter of May 4,
says the Yugoslav leaders "have pierced every one's ears by
their unlimited self-praise"; he goes on, the only reason
the Italian and French Communists did not do as well as the
Yugoslavs is that the Soviet army could not get to Italy and
France to put them in power. This is a striking admission,
and the way it slips out is evidence of Stalin's rage: it implies
that the Communist governments in eastern Europe were
all made by the Soviet army and not, as the Russians claimed,
by the will of the people. There is an even more striking
proof that Stalin's rage has got the better of him. To counter
Tito's reference to his past successes, Stalin writes: "In his
time Trotsky, too, rendered revolutionary services" but later
became an enemy of the Soviet Union. That is an astonishing
confession: for twenty years Trotsky's name has not been
mentioned in the Soviet Union except as a term of abuse,
and he does not appear in the standard histories of the revolution. Now Stalin blurts out: Trotsky too rendered revolutionary
services. He has not quite got to the point yet of saying that
they were second only to those of Lenin.

Tito's crime is to be independent: he demands to be treated as an equal. He writes to Stalin as one Communist ruler to another; he bargains with the Soviet Communist party and refuses to appear before the Cominform. His worst crime is to refuse to allow the Soviet intelligence service to recruit members inside Yugoslavia; he actually dogs the Soviet secret police with secret police of his own. That shows that the essential conflict is a conflict of power and authority, not of doctrine. So far as doctrine goes Tito is by no means a heretic. Far from it—he, Kardelj and the others are the most orthodox believers. They protest in their letters that in no country is there so much Communist teaching, nowhere are there sold so many copies of Stalin's works. As they rightly observe, people don't read Stalin's works for pleasure: they read them only if they have them rammed down their throats —"stubbornly inculcated" is the phrase they use. Tito, in fact, is not Luther; he is Henry VIII. Henry VIII, too, was strictly orthodox in point of doctrine, indeed Defender of the Faith; only he wanted to be his own Pope. Long after he had quarrelled with Rome, Henry was burning heretics at Smith-field; and non-Communists still have a rough time in Yugo-slavia. All the same, once Henry VIII broke with Rome, Protestantism was inevitable: the only appeal from dogmatic authority is to the judgment of the individual. Tito is following the same path. The other day he said again that truth [meaning himself] is above authority [meaning Stalin] and denounced the doctrine that the end justifies the means. But this doctrine is essential to Communism, as it was to militant Catholicism; otherwise you must admit that moral values like truth justice, tolerance, are more important than the Church or the Cominform.

The analogy with Henry VIII raises a further question in regard to Tito. When Henry VIII defied the Papacy he could rely on the rising national feeling in England and on the "new men" who grew wealthy from commerce and land-speculation. What is there behind Tito? Not merely a secret police—though that is the most important thing when you are up against Stalin and the Soviet Union. Not merely "new men"—the young Communists who fought the partisan war and now fill the army and the administration, "new men" for whom "Hero-Tito" personifies their own achievements against the Germans. Nor is it enough to talk, as the Stalinists and others do, of "narrow nationalism." If Tito's stand were merely nationalistic, he would be backed by the Serbs and no one else. In reality he is not supported more by one nationality in Yugoslavia than another. Yugoslavia is not a national state: it is a federation of peoples, in which there is no longer national privilege or advantage. Of course the Yugoslavs are proud of their country. As Tito says in his most subversive sentence—a sentence for which alone the Communists will send him to the stake: "No matter how much each of us loves the land of Socialism, you cannot ask him to love his own country less." But they are proud of their country, partly because it is an association of peoples, quite as much as the Soviet Union itself; indeed, more so—the Russians are the "people of state" in the Soviet Union far more than the Serbs are the "people of state" in Yugoslavia. In a curious roundabout way, "federal, democratic Yugoslavia"—the official name of Tito's State—is an attempt to realize the international dream which was supposed to lie behind the old Austrian Empire, the Habsburg Monarchy: to discover for the peoples of central and eastern Europe a political order which would be neither German nor Russian, but something in between. Tito, in fact, is the heir of the Habsburgs; and the conflict between Tito and Stalin is a new version of the old conflict between Habsburg and Romanov. Only the Habsburgs never found a real mission with which to justify their Empire, except simply the claims of dynastic right. More fortunate than the Habsburgs, Tito has found an "idea": Yugoslavia is a country which believes in itself.

After Tito's declaration of independence there can never be a reconciliation between him and orthodox Communism. That does not necessarily mean he is done for. Though Stalin and his associates are crazy with power, they will hardly overthrow Tito in order to restore capitalism in Yugoslavia —and that is likely to be the alternative. Nor is it to our interest to pull Tito over to the West, as some people seem to long to do. I do not believe the world situation is improved by everyone being compelled to line up with one or other of the giants, Russia or America. Quite the contrary: the more countries are independent of both, the better. The best outcome for all the eastern European countries would be Communist states independent of Moscow and cheeking Moscow as Tito does. More: the best thing for us and for the world in general is that we should be America's Tito.

XIV

TWO CONGRESSES

(1) *The Paris Congress of the History of* 1848

A NATION reveals its character in the way it seeks to impress foreigners. The Russians used to show visitors factories, in the days when they had visitors; in England we take visitors to a football match or, more grudgingly, to Stratford; the sights of America are Hollywood and Niagara, or perhaps nowadays the distant prospect of an atomic-bomb plant. Only the French would demonstrate their "way of life" by organizing a serious Congress of Historians to mark the centenary of the revolutions of 1848. In England an historian is regarded as an impractical pedant, a tiresome necessity for teaching the young, and the title of "professor" is a disqualification for public life. In France a professor, and especially a professor of history, enjoys the standing and influence of an elder statesman, and every historian assumes that his work contributes to the public life of France.

The Congress for the study of the history of the revolutions of 1848 was a formidable affair—formidable in the number of those who attended it and also both in the number and in the quality of the papers that were read.

The composition of the Congress itself revealed something of the position which France seeks to occupy in Europe. There were no American historians and no Russians; the two Great Powers who brawl across the half-conscious body of Europe were both absent from this essentially European commemoration. The few British historians were present as private observers, not as delegates; this, too, was symbolic of our equivocal attitude to Europe, half in, half out. The small countries who have looked to France in the past for inspiration and sometimes for protection were present in force: there were delegations from Norway, Denmark,

Belgium, Holland and Switzerland. Of the countries behind the "iron curtain" only the Hungarians arrived on time: the Czechs were one day late, the Poles three—another agreeable symbol. The countries of western Europe repeated the French version of 1848—that is, their delegates talked almost exclusively of national independence and individual liberty. The Hungarians contributed something new in a social analysis of their revolutions; this infuriated the Czechs, who insisted on the national conflicts of 1848. The Czechs, in fact, clung to an old-fashioned "western" approach; the Hungarians are preparing to be the equal partners of the Russians, as they once were of the Germans and before that of the Habsburgs.

There was one Austrian, who remained silent. Apart from him, the Germans were not represented; and it would have been possible to sit through the Congress almost without becoming aware that there had been an earth-shaking revolution in Germany in 1848. This revealed a deep weakness in French politics of the present. Always conscious of the German problem, they see no solution of it and, therefore, try to ignore it. Their vision of Europe is still that of small countries clustered round France, a vision far from reality. This French vision was challenged at the congress by the Italians, who alone disputed the French version of 1848. The Italians claimed, as it were, equality with France and Great Power status. Indeed, they went further and asserted the primacy of the Italian revolutions of 1848. In their view the spirit of 1848 was most clearly expressed by Mazzini and it was his doctrine of nationalism which carried the day in eastern Europe.

The Italians went further than the French in denying the economic character of the revolutions of 1848; for them the revolutions sprang from idealistic, intellectual causes. The French historians were too serious to accept this one-sided explanation. Some of their contributions to economic history were novel and first rate. Still, even they were more concerned with why the revolution took place than with why it failed. The emphasis was all on universal suffrage and on liberty of expression. In exalting the Second Republic the

Fourth Republic is exalting itself. The analogy is depressingly close. In the "June Days" the Second Republic defeated the social movement of the working-classes as the Fourth Republic has defeated the Communists (though not with the same bloodshed). The effort exhausted the radicalism of the Second Republic and it fell before a half-Socialist, half-military adventurer, Louis Napoleon; the Fourth Republic feels at its back the breath of another strong man, de Gaulle. It was curious how little attention the Congress gave to the working-class movement and to the social problem. No doubt by chance, the only paper on the June Days was a discussion by a retired general on the technical military problems raised by the preparations for civil war; it was almost the most remarkable paper of the Congress.

On more than one occasion the French historians raised what one might call "the English problem." Why, they asked, was there no revolution in England in 1848? What was the secret which enabled the English governing classes to take the workers into partnership without violence and without destroying individual freedom? I am afraid that we English historians did little to enlighten them. Yet this is for European civilization the question of existence, raised in 1848 and not yet answered. On the continent of Europe, though perhaps less in this country, the outlook which we now call democratic and which used to be called liberal is held only by a minority of educated men. Government by free discussion; toleration of opponents; the security of the individual; and the rule of law—these causes have never commanded mass support. They have been tolerated, no more, and in order to be tolerated they have had to offer the masses prosperity. They have been luxuries, the first casualties in time of foreign danger or domestic distress. Perhaps they were secure only so long as Europe lived on the tribute of the other continents.

Still, the Congress—like countless other meetings of a similar nature—was a demonstration that European civilization exists. The historians from every country approached their problems in the same way, with the same honesty and the same devotion; all, except the hosts, spoke the same language—bad French. Europe may be divided politically at the "iron curtain"; it cannot be divided culturally. This European civilization deserves something better than to become the pawn of the Great Powers. The Congress illustrated sharply, though on a small scale, the two problems which must be solved if European civilization is to survive: Germany must be brought back into civilized Europe; and the masses must be persuaded that this civilization belongs also to them. The French see these problems; they have not found the solution. English people are stumbling towards a solution without seeing the problems; that was the pattern of 1848. England and France together might give Europe a new chance of life. Certainly European civilization will be ruined if it is "saved" by either Russia or America.

(2) *The Wroclaw Congress of Intellectuals*

Julien Benda, who was himself at Wroclaw, must have acquired new material for "The Treason of the Intellectuals." This treason was of two kinds: the treason of the Communist, who is prepared to sacrifice liberty and intellectual standards for the victory of his party, and—far graver—the treason of the well-meaning fellow-travellers, who suppose that the Russians can be won over by soft words and one-sided gestures of goodwill. The Congress originated as just such a gesture: it was suggested by some Polish artists and taken up by French writers (including M. Benda) as a genuine attempt to lessen international tension by bringing men of culture together. The Poles, in fact, are as reluctant to be dragged along the road of conflict by Russia as the French are to be dragged along the same road by the United States. In financing the Congress (and I calculate it must have cost £100,000) the Polish Government had a practical political object: alarmed by the reluctance of the Western Powers to recognize the Oder-Neisse Line, they wished to establish the world fame of "the ancient Polish city" of Wroclaw and to blot out all recollection of Breslau. Hence even a few tame German Communists were brought in to grace this Polish holiday. For my part I hope that this object has been attained; and I only regret that it should be necessary to spend £100,000 to extract from the West the acknowledgment of Polish rights that honour and interest alike should dictate to us.

The British and American guests had then ground for believing that the Congress would offer a real opportunity for cultural co-operation; and Julian Huxley came from Paris with the same hope. Such a Congress would have been the most effective Communist propaganda. The Communists blundered from dogmatic stupidity and from an inability to act honestly even when they wished to. Though the British "delegation" (delegated, of course, by nobody) was invited with reasonable fairness, the French and Italian delegations were packed with Communists: Gide, Mauriac and Sartre, for example, were not invited. Moreover Mr. Borejsza, the Polish dictator of culture who organized the Congress, was not thinking in terms of practical intellectual co-operation or even of serious discussion: the Congress (like the Parliaments of the "new democracies") was to listen to a series of prepared speeches, reiterating the same theme in an exhausting process of mass hypnosis and reaching a climax in a unanimous resolution against American Fascism. Uniformity and unanimity are essentials of Communist culture; and it was self-evident to the Communists that the Congress should proceed in this way and no other.

The Communist pattern of the Congress had two sides: first, interminable speeches by representatives of colonial peoples oppressed by western Imperialism, then equally interminable speeches by representatives of peoples liberated by the Soviet Union. No one pointed out that the representatives of the oppressed coloured peoples for the most part make a snug living out of their oppressors as successful intellectuals in London or Paris. Altogether we had eleven oppressed peoples (or twelve if you count the British fellow-travellers groaning under American Imperialism) and ten liberated peoples. When we got to Azerbaijan I thought we were to have all the peoples of the Soviet Union; fortunately the supply of intellectuals ran short at this point.

Boredom alone would not have led to revolt. The Communists' false move was to launch the Congress with a speech by the Russian novelist Fadeyev. It was evidence of Soviet culture, he claimed, that he had sold two million copies of his novel in the last two years. His speech was what one might expect from the writer of a crude best-seller, and the effect of it could not be undone even by a sophisticated performance by Ilya Ehrenburg the following day. British writers, even of the Left, resented the attack on T. S. Eliot, a welcome display of professional solidarity; and some even disliked the assertion that the Soviet Union had won the last war without assistance.

The material for resistance was slight. The few French non-Communists would not co-operate; and apart from a quiet statement by M. Benda (now over eighty) the Congress heard no French voice raised in defence of the Rights of Man. It was characteristic of the decline of France that the French, having failed to defend intellectual freedom, should quieten their consciences by proposing a mass visit to Ausschwitz. Of the British "delegation" sixteen were Communists and others were Marxist sympathizers. Professor Hyman Levy, for instance, dismissed as "fantastic" the claim that the issue of intellectual freedom was of any importance. The British Communists, I suppose, relied on the big guns —Professors Bernal and Haldane and the Dean of Canterbury —which they held in reserve; but their reluctance to allow anyone to speak in opposition was swept away by Mr. Kingsley Martin who, with his usual gaiety of spirit, wanted some stir and excitement in exchange for the efforts he had made in coming to Wroclaw (even if a day late).

Though a speech in favour of intellectual freedom and mutual understanding did not disturb Russian complacency, it ruined the effect of unanimity which they had hoped to achieve. The Americans had at first been contented to make speeches explaining why they supported Henry Wallace; as one of them said, if only America were a true democracy (he must have meant a new democracy) Wallace would be elected. Before the end of the Congress Mr. Bryn Hovde, of New York, spoke out too for freedom; his appeal that we should work together was met with heavy silence from all except a handful of English and Americans.

More serious, from the Russian point of view, was the failure to reach an agreed resolution, despite three days of intrigue and deception (including the alteration of an agreed draft while it was being duplicated): the existence of a dissenting minority had to be announced throughout the new democracy. The British dissenters displayed glorious individualism to the last. Three, Edward Crankshaw, Denis Saurat and myself, made a public statement to the press; four others were willing to record their dissent in the *Manchester Guardian*, but not to an American reporter. Six more signed the statement and then withdrew their signatures when they learned that it was intended for publication; I suppose they thought we were collecting autographs. However, in intellectual conflict numbers are of no importance; conviction is all that matters.

The Russians certainly acted from conviction, not only in their principles but equally, I am sure, in the sincere conviction that the Soviet Union stands in immediate peril of attack from the United States. For them it is urgent to rally their satellites. The Russians are entitled to defend their convictions. Western intellectuals ought to have stood up for theirs and tried to restore a culture which is neither Soviet nor American but the heritage of all humanity. If the British, French and Americans had been genuinely represented the Congress could have had immeasurable effect, as the private comment of Czechs, Poles and others showed. The fault lies with British intellectuals who were invited to Wroclaw and would not trouble to go. Their place was taken by such as Professor Haldane, who won easy applause with the statement, "If people in England are planning a war against Poland it is like kicking a woman in labour" and "We are rebuilding London slower than you are rebuilding Wroclaw because we are spending so much on war preparations."

All the same, it is something that uniformity was not achieved. Metternich said at Aix-la-Chapelle: "I have never seen a prettier little Congress." The Russians will not say this of Wroclaw.